NEW
BATHROOM
IDEA BOOK

ANDREW WORMER

The Taunton Press

To little Willem

The Taunton Press
Inspiration for hands-on living®

The Taunton Press, Inc., 63 South Main Street, PO Box 5506, Newtown, CT 06470-5506
e-mail: tp@taunton.com

New Bathroom Idea Book was originally published in hardcover
in 2004 by The Taunton Press, Inc.

EDITOR: Stefanie Ramp
JACKET DESIGN: Jeannet Leendertse
INTERIOR DESIGN: Lori Wendin
LAYOUT: Cathy Cassidy
ILLUSTRATOR: Christine Erikson
COVER PHOTOGRAPHERS: Front cover, top row (left to right): © Lee Brauer Photography; Charles Miller
© The Taunton Press, Inc., Charles Bickford © The Taunton Press, Inc.; © davidduncanlivingston.com;
second row: © Mark Samu; © davidduncanlivingston.com; © Tim Street-Porter; third row: © Brian Vanden Brink,
Photographer 2003; Charles Miller © The Taunton Press, Inc.; © Hester & Hardaway; © Brian Vanden Brink,
Photographer 2003; Back cover, top: © Jason McConathy; bottom row (left to right): Roe Osborn © The Taunton
Press, Inc.; © Tim Street-Porter; Roe Osborn © The Taunton Press, Inc.

Taunton Home® is a trademark of The Taunton Press, Inc.,
registered in the U.S. Patent and Trademark Office.

Library of Congress Cataloging-in-Publication Data
Wormer, Andrew.
  New bathroom idea book / Andrew Wormer.
      p. cm.
  ISBN 1-56158-643-9 hardcover
  ISBN 1-56158-692-7 paperback
  1. Bathrooms--Remodeling. I. Title.
  TH4816 .W6724 2004
  747.7'8--dc21
                            2003013591

Printed in the United States of America
10 9 8 7 6 5

The following manufacturers/names appearing in *New Bathroom Idea Book* are trademarks:
Anaglypta™, Avonite®, Briggs® (Vacuity®), CaesarStone®, Corian®, Formica® (Surell® and Ligna®), Jacuzzi®, Kohler®,
National Kitchen and Bath Association (NKBA)®, Runtal®, Silestone®, Swanstone™, Syndecrete™, Toto®, Trespa™, Vola®,
Wilsonart® (Gibraltar® and Earthstone™), Y-Slip™, Zodiaq™.

Acknowledgments

When Peter Chapman, senior developmental editor at Taunton Press, called me last year to propose a new edition of *The Bathroom Idea Book*, I thought that he was joking. After all, it seemed to me that the book had just appeared (though in fact it had been published way back in 1999), and that at least a couple of more years could pass before it was time to revisit this material. But once I started looking closely at the new photographs that I was receiving from the professional photographers who contributed to this book, I realized that Peter's take on timing was just about right. So, thanks to Peter for helping to get me into this mess. And thanks to all of those other talented folks at Taunton—especially editor Stefanie Ramp and senior managing editor Carolyn Mandarano—for helping to get me out of it. Without their expertise and good advice, this book would remain just a good idea.

The beautiful photography that makes this book possible comes from a variety of sources. Architectural photography—and bathroom photography in particular—is a challenge, and I'm fortunate to be able to rely once again on the work of some of the best in the business. Not to be underestimated is the contribution of current and past staff members of Fine Homebuilding magazine; many of the projects and photographs featured in this book first appeared in its pages. I particularly appreciate the opportunity to reprint the photographs taken by such folks as Kevin Ireton, Chuck Miller, Roe Osborn, Scott Gibson, Andy Engel, and Chuck Bickford; they've all developed a remarkable talent for capturing telling architectural detail on film. The National Kitchen and Bath Association (NKBA)® also generously contributed photography; anyone considering a project in these two areas would be well advised to start their research with a visit to the NKBA Web site. Each of these individual photographers is credited by name in the back of the book, but my special thanks to all of you.

Of course, none of the bathrooms featured in these pages would be possible without the design skills of the people who conceived them and the construction skills of the people who built them. Whenever possible, I've tried to credit both the designer and builder of each bathroom, and my special thanks to all of those who have taken the extra time to explain their ideas, provide information about materials and fixtures, and offer general design advice. Unfortunately, in many cases the tradespeople—carpenters, plumbers, electricians, tile setters, cabinetmakers, painters, and other artisans—who actually built these bathrooms remain anonymous, though not intentionally so. As one who has dabbled in all of these trades (with varying degrees of success), my hat is off to you.

Finally, thanks to my family for their understanding while I remained hunkered down out here in my office, surrounded by files and boxes and mountains of photographs. They've waited a long time for me to stop writing about bathrooms and start doing something about 'em. So, one down, and one (or two) more to go.

Contents

Introduction

The other morning I returned from the hardware store with a gallon of paint, one of the finishing touches for the bathroom that I've been renovating in our house while concurrently working on this sequel to *The Bathroom Idea Book*. Like this new edition of the book, my bathroom has been under construction for a while. Driving into town for more supplies or wrestling for a couple of hours with some part of the job before or after sitting down at the computer for the day has become a familiar ritual. In fact, I began breaking out tile from our old, leaky shower eight months ago at about the same time I began sorting in earnest through the piles of new photographs that photographers had been sending me.

This morning I painted a test patch on one of the bathroom walls to see how it looks. My idea is to have bright, cheerful, blue upper walls over white wainscot in order to keep this rather traditionally appointed bathroom from looking boring to the kids who will mostly use it. But I'm not so sure about the blue—it's *very* bright.

Both the book and my bathroom have been demanding more than an equal share of my attention over the past year. This has benefited them both, I think. I've been able to incorporate a lot of the ideas that I've written about in this book into our compact bathroom. And the process of planning and building the bathroom has been a great help in writing the book, as it's prompted me to reexamine the decision-making process that accompanies any bathroom project.

I make this note about the paint because in my experience as a builder of many bathrooms this symbolic finale to the construction process is one of the decisions most agonized over. My guess is that my family will take more notice of the final coat of paint than any other phase of this bathroom's extensive gut and rebuild. Stripping out walls down to the studs and floors down to the joists and removing toilets and sinks is cool, sure, but changing the color of the bathroom is what will really catch their attention.

I've had to make literally dozens of decisions—about materials, about layout, about fixtures—in the building of this

bathroom. Fortunately, the paint is one decision that's easy to correct with a couple of hours of labor and a gallon of something else. But I'm confident about the overall design because I've invested time and energy into choosing the fixtures and materials that are right for this bathroom. I'm confident we'll get the colors right too.

You'll need to make these same kinds of decisions as you build or renovate your own bathroom. I think you'll find this book an invaluable guide; use it both as a source for inspiration and as a practical reference as you make decisions about layout, materials, and fixtures. With this book in hand you won't be alone as you sweat the details and get the big picture. I'm betting you'll get the colors right, too.

Designing a Great Bathroom

ATHROOM DESIGN used to be a simple affair back when fixtures were available in only a few styles and colors and the sole purpose of a bathroom was to provide a room for personal hygiene. Because of its utilitarian nature, this room was sized to fit only a toilet, tub, and sink, with little space to spare. But bathrooms have evolved; they're bigger now and play multiple roles, from therapeutic spa for the whole family to personal refuge to workout area. That makes for bathrooms that are far more interesting and attractive, but it makes bathroom design a bit more complicated.

Where to begin? One way is to start window-shopping for fixtures, visiting showrooms and home centers, and putting your Web browser to good use. This is a great way to see the range of features and styles that are available in bathing fixtures, toilets, and lavatories, and to get you thinking about which are important to you and your family, and which you can do without. I think you'll be amazed at your options.

But good bathroom design is about more than bells and whistles. Before you spring for a luxurious whirlpool tub or a glamorous above-counter glass sink, you need to ask some important questions. Who will be using the bathroom? How often? Where will it be located? How big will it be? How much do you want to spend? The answers to these questions will help guide you as you make decisions about fixtures, materials, layout, and style.

◀ LOCATED IN A RESTORED VICTORIAN HOUSE on the Massachusetts coast, this classic bath features a Carrara marble floor and modern fixtures with a period look. But unlike the old bathrooms that this master bath intentionally resembles, this one has plenty of storage, with two generously sized, custom-built medicine cabinets and a built-in, glass-front linen closet.

▲ LOCATED IN A RESTORED 1950s vintage ranch house on the grounds of the Shelburne Museum in Vermont, this family bathroom is authentic right down to the pink fixtures and matching vinyl window and shower curtains.

▶ ONE WELCOME TREND IN BATH-ROOM DESIGN is to borrow ideas from different cultures. This Japanese-style bath features a deep soaking tub and an open shower tucked beneath the rafters. Note the two drains in the tiled floor to collect splashes in both the shower and tub area.

DEFINING THE BATH

Chances are you already have a pretty good idea of where the bathroom will be located, who will be using it, and how much space will be available for it. With this information, you can define the type of bath that it will be—compact bath, master bath, children's bath, or guest bath—and begin making decisions about fixtures and finishes that are appropriate for the space. For example, a master bathroom may be part of a larger suite, so choices about finishes will likely reflect the decor in the bedroom and dressing areas. In a compact bath—that is, an all-purpose bathroom intended for use by a range of family members—durability and ease of maintenance are key issues.

◄MODERN MASTER BATHS TYPICALLY ARE LARGE, resulting in more flexible and relaxed layouts. This one features a marble countertop and limestone floors, a big walk-in shower, and a separate soaking tub. Designed to make the most of natural light while still providing privacy, these generous windows have a sandblasted finish on the lower two-thirds.

How Far Will Your Money Go?

- **$1,000 and under:** Cosmetic surgery—new paint, perhaps a new toilet and/or sink—can go a long way toward giving your bathroom a new outlook. Other options: new flooring; new tub or shower door.

- **$1,000 to $2,500:** Plan on keeping the same layout, but you'll be able to install a new toilet and sink. Another possibility is to replace the tub or shower.

- **$2,500 to $7,500:** A new suite of fixtures and new floors and finish materials are a possibility, as long as you don't make major floor-plan changes.

- **$7,500 to $12,000:** Most major bathroom rehabs—with a gutted interior, new fixture locations, perhaps a new window or skylight—fall in this price range.

- **$12,000 to $20,000:** A basic remodel can quickly jump into this price range—and beyond—when using premium fixtures or materials. Major architectural changes like a bump-out or closet conversion can also quickly add to the cost of a project.

▲CLUTTER IS ONE CHARACTERISTIC COMMON to bathrooms used by kids. One way to help kids keep control over the many items that they use in a bathroom is to provide plenty of easily accessed storage space, like these above-the-counter cubbies.

▲ELIMINATING AN EXTRA—and unnecessary—sink in the vanity makes room for both a tub and separate shower in this no-nonsense bath. The simple fixtures are dressed up by the glazed and painted walls and stenciled autumn leaves.

▲ LIKE MANY COMPACT BATHROOMS, this one has to work for both kids and adults, and it packs a lot of storage and style into its simple 48-sq.-ft. rectangular footprint. The vintage claw-foot tub and pedestal sink were refinished with a spray-applied, two-part epoxy paint, while the flooring is a mixture of salvaged roofing slate and bargain-basement white ceramic tile.

◄ THIS LONG, NARROW BATHROOM looks wider thanks to the horizontal sight lines created by the glass countertop and different paint colors. The large mirror helps to give this compact room the illusion of depth.

Compact Family Baths

Probably the hardest-working room in the house, a bathroom that serves an entire family has more demands placed on it than any other type of bathroom. For one thing, these bathrooms typically have limited floor space available, usually 5 ft. by 9 ft. or less. With space at a premium, you'll need to give careful consideration to planning fixture locations and providing adequate storage.

Another factor to be considered is that bathrooms like these are in almost constant use, particularly if there are teens in the family. You'll want to choose fixtures and materials that are both durable and easily cleaned. Unfortunately, you'll find that quality—a solid brass ceramic-disc faucet versus a less-expensive model, for example—comes at a price. In the long run, though, the extra initial expense will more than pay for itself.

◄ SIMPLE STYLING AND NATURAL MATERIALS give this small bath an understated, Far East flavor, a look enhanced by the travertine countertop holding the vessel-style marble bowl, the tarnished copper backsplash, and the multicolored river-stone border on the tumbled-slate floor.

► THE BROKEN EDGE DETAIL ON THIS SMALL, square bathroom's marble wall tile injects an element of drama and adds volume to the room.

A Basement Bathroom

BASEMENT BATHROOMS offer some special—but not insurmountable—challenges. The first is a question of drainage, as most waste lines exit the basement above the level of the floor. This can be corrected with the addition of a sewage pump buried below slab level. While there are several different types available from different manufacturers, they basically consist of a pump inside a holding tank; when the drainage from the bathroom's fixtures reaches a preset level within the tank, the pump kicks on, flushing the contents up and into the house's main sewer line.

A second challenge is low headroom and the absence of natural light. If there is a window, of course, take advantage of it and try to emphasize its size. Be sure that artificial lighting more than compensates for the lack of daylight. And try to avoid horizontal lines, instead emphasizing vertical lines—for example, extending tile finishes and cabinetry all the way to the ceiling, which draws the eye upward. Finally, choose light colors to help amplify the effects of both natural and artificial lighting.

▲ THOUGH THIS BASEMENT BATHROOM ISN'T LARGE, it features a spacious walk-in shower with off-white tile, a generous overhead fixture, and translucent-glass shower doors.

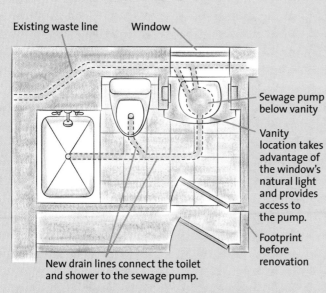

Existing waste line   Window

Sewage pump below vanity

Vanity location takes advantage of the window's natural light and provides access to the pump.

Footprint before renovation

New drain lines connect the toilet and shower to the sewage pump.

Once a utilitarian space housing only a toilet installed on a raised platform, this bathroom's footprint was reduced slightly to make better use of the existing space. Adding a new sewage pump buried beneath the floor allows the bathroom to utilize conventionally installed fixtures.

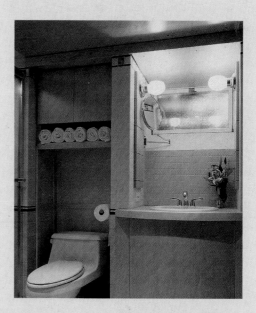

▲ A BUILT-IN MAPLE CABINET in the toilet alcove extends all the way to the ceiling of this basement bathroom, adding much-needed storage and emphasizing the vertical dimension.

Master Bath Suites

Bathrooms that serve a single bedroom don't usually have the same space constraints as a compact bath; consequently, their design can be driven by whim as much as by necessity. In many cases it is easier to "borrow" space if necessary from the adjacent sleeping area. In fact, many master bathrooms benefit from compartmentalizing different functions so that there may be a separate toilet stall, a dressing area, and a bathing area all integrated within the overall plan.

Master baths can afford to be the most idiosyncratic type of bathroom, a perfect place to try new ideas and think outside the box. But keep in mind that practicality should also be an important component in the design; ultimately, a master bath should be planned in a way that best serves the individual or couple using it. For some, this means a shower large enough for two; for others, this means discrete spaces that afford some privacy while being used simultaneously.

▶ WHILE THIS MASTER BATH isn't particularly large, the high peaked ceiling and creative use of reflective surfaces make it feel spacious. A slate floor, black polished granite countertops, and a planting area behind the soaking tub (shown here reflected in the mirror) help keep this bathroom connected to the natural world.

▲SLIDING SCREENS SEPARATE THIS BATHING AREA from the adjacent bedroom. The screens can be closed for privacy or opened to a view of the bedroom's fireplace or television.

Creating Space

ONE OF THE BIGGEST CHALLENGES in bathroom design is adequate space. Using smaller fixtures—a shower instead of a full-size tub, for example—is one of the easiest solutions, while some fixtures can be eliminated altogether. Do you really need a bidet or an extra sink? A second option is to annex space from an adjoining area, such as a closet, hallway, or bedroom. When all else fails, create space. Converting unused space—an attic above a garage, for example—is one possibility, as is building an addition. However, a money-saving alternative is a bump-out; exterior walls can often be bumped out as much as 2 ft. without a foundation.

▲AN OVERSIZED CLAW-FOOT SOAKING TUB is the centerpiece of this light-filled master bath. The vaulted ceiling gives a spacious feeling to the room, which has a large walk-in shower to the left. While the look is antique, all of the fixtures are reproductions.

▶CRAFTSMAN-STYLE DETAILING distinguishes this master bath, including a custom-built tablelike vanity with open storage beneath. The unfitted character of the vanity and the warm wood tones create a pleasing contrast with the cool, hard surface of the tiled floor and wainscot.

▲THOUGH NOT PARTICULARLY LARGE, this master bath has lots of storage thanks to the built-in linen cabinet and shelving over the tub. Details like the Carrara marble floor and tub deck, and beaded wainscot hint at the home's Victorian architecture.

▶WHEN PLANNING A MASTER BATH, try to organize the space by functions, giving each a separate area rather than simply lining up the fixtures against the walls. Here, the tub alcove functions like a separate room with its own storage, adjacent to but discreet from the centrally located vanity.

Seaside Bath

On Martha's Vineyard off the Massachusetts coast, outdoor showers are a popular—and enjoyable—way of washing off sand and salt water after a day at the beach. With its teak deck boards and partitions and open arrangement, this master bath recreates that feeling year-round. Roughly 10 ft. by 10 ft., this squarish room is divided into four quadrants by a simple shower curtain and two curved, slatted, teak and stainless-steel partitions, providing each area of the bathroom with a degree of privacy while retaining the views toward the nearby ocean. Big windows over the tub and mirrors over the vanity, toilet, and bidet enhance the spacious feeling of this modestly sized bathroom, providing panoramic views of Vineyard Sound from every corner of the room.

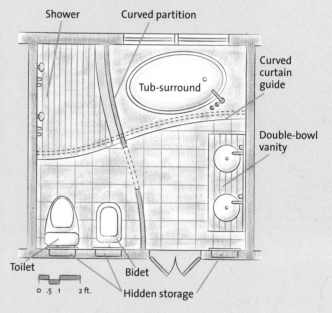

Wavelike curved partitions built with stainless steel and laminated teak divide this seaside bath into four separate quadrants. Natural light and views of the ocean enter the room through the windows over the tub and are reflected all around the room by a number of mirrors.

Shower · Curved partition · Curved curtain guide · Tub-surround · Double-bowl vanity · Toilet · Bidet · Hidden storage

0 .5 1 2 ft.

◄ TEAK DECK BOARDS UNDERFOOT and a curved teak partition between the shower and soaking tub give this island bathroom a nautical feel. The tub deck is tiled with ocean-green tumbled-marble mosaics.

▲ PLAYFUL TRIM TILE AND BRIGHT BLUE WALLS jazz up this mostly-white bathroom, infusing it with both fun and sophistication. Located low and near the door, the shower controls can be operated from both inside and outside the shower, a good safety feature for both kids and adults.

Children's Baths

Bathrooms intended for use almost exclusively by children are a relatively recent phenomenon, but the principles that guide their design—safety, appropriate scale, and practical fun—can be applied to any bathroom that kids might use.

Probably the biggest obstacle that children face when using any bathroom is simply reaching to sinks that are sized for adults. A step stool is a simple solution, but another option is to lower the sink. Durable, water-resistant surfaces everywhere are another good idea in a children's bathroom. And don't forget plenty of easily accessible storage, ranging from waterproof bins for toddler's bath toys to drawers and shelves for teen's cosmetics. These are the kinds of considerations that make designated children's baths—and family bathrooms that are used by children—work better.

◀ THE WALLS OF THIS SHOWER are finished with solid-surfacing, a material that is both durable and easy to clean—a good combination for a family with kids.

Safety for Children

BATHROOMS POSE A SPECIAL RISK to small children. Here are some steps you can take to reduce that risk:

- Turn your home's hot water temperature down to 120° F. Water heaters are often set to temperatures as high as 150° F, which can cause an instant third-degree burn on a child.
- Keep medicines and cleaning products out of bathrooms used by children.
- Don't leave children unattended in a tub.
- Remember that toilets present a drowning hazard to toddlers; toilet locks are available to reduce the risk.

◀ ONCE DULL AND DREARY, this bathroom has been transformed into a colorful children's bath by painting and reorienting the tub and moving fixture locations to open up the center of the room. The playful tile murals are hand-made and installed against a background of relatively inexpensive, commercially available tile.

▲▶ THE INTRICATE, HANDMADE, CERAMIC MOSAIC TILES that decorate this shower stall (above) and matching countertop backsplash (right) turn a visit to the bathroom into a mini-vacation to the Caribbean.

A Bathroom for All Ages

WHILE IT MAY NOT SEEM LIKE IT SOMETIMES, **children grow quickly; keep that in mind if you're designing a bathroom intended to be used** primarily by children. This cheerful bathroom features fun—but not juvenile—colors and an inviting full-size shower stall that makes it a little easier to coax the little ones into clean-up mode, but it's a full-featured adult bathroom as well.

For example, the mirror over the sink tilts so that it can be easily seen by all sizes. The body sprays in the shower are a fun and practical way for kids to get clean, and are supplemented by a hand-held shower and a fixed-height showerhead sized for an adult. The controls are all easily reached by kids, and a securely attached grab bar in the shower makes bathing safer for everyone. Thanks to the exterior glass-block window and the interior translucent partition window and shower door, this bathroom is light and bright, a quality appreciated by all ages.

▲A TILTING MIRROR LIKE THIS is a simple, kid-friendly addition to any bathroom. Bright colors and a simple yet sophisticated design make the space enjoyable and functional for users of all ages.

▲A GLASS-BLOCK WINDOW IN THE SHOWER STALL lets in plenty of natural light while an acid-etched interior window brightens the rest of the room.

◀A BODY SPRAY IS A GREAT ADDITION to a kid's bath. This one is located only 38 in. above the floor and regulated by a thermostatic valve to prevent scalding.

▲ DESIGNED TO FEEL LIKE AN OLD ITALIAN VILLA, this powder room features a floor of imported tumbled limestone and plaster walls highlighted by a 17th-century French tapestry and an 18th-century French gilded mirror over the sink.

Guest Baths & Powder Rooms

In most cases, guest baths are used relatively infrequently, so durability is not as much of an issue in this type of bathroom. Exquisite fixtures and finishes aren't at risk from moisture damage (because there is no bath or shower) or from harsh cleaning chemicals, so materials can be chosen based more on how they look than on how well they'll stand up to abuse.

Because a guest bath is more of a public space than other types of bathrooms, you'll want to consider carefully how its appearance reflects the style and architecture of the rest of your home. Here is where a flair for the dramatic comes in handy and can be indulged.

▲ THOUGH SMALL, this powder room features plenty of storage both above and below the floating granite countertop. The ceramic checkerboard backsplash and monochromatic color scheme were chosen to match materials and colors in the nearby hallway.

▼THE LIMESTONE FLOOR and pan-eled wainscot of the adjacent foyer extend into this powder room, giving it a formal elegance matched by the dark limestone countertop and curved-front vanity.

►LOCATED NOT IN A HOUSE but in a historical passenger train, this tiny bath features a corner-mounted sink to take advantage of the limited space; the floor-to-ceiling mirror next to the sink makes the room feel larger.

Private Matters

DOORWAYS FOR GUEST BATHS and pow-der rooms should be planned so that there's a transition area between the private space of the bathroom and a very public space, such as a kitchen or great room. When possible, these doorways should open into a hallway or smaller room (such as a den or guest bedroom). It's also a good idea to place the toilet out of the line of sight of an open door, either by situat-ing the fixture behind the door when it's open or in a separate nook.

BATHROOM PLANNING

Once the bathroom's basic footprint and purpose have been determined, you'll need to figure out how best to organize the actual and apparent space. Will there be room for both a tub and a shower? Where is the best place for the toilet? How can a small space be made to feel larger? In any successful bath design the space shouldn't look or feel cramped, even though it may be small.

As the design evolves you'll want to choose materials that look good, are durable, and enhance the overall appearance of the bathroom. You'll also want to plan your bathroom so that it is safe and accessible for all of your family members.

▲ MANY BATHROOMS CAN BE DIVIDED by function, allowing more family members to use them simultaneously. Here a pocket door separates the bath/shower area from the lavatory which helps preserve the spacious feeling of this moderately sized bathroom.

▶ SEPARATED FROM THE REST OF THE ROOM by its own alcove, this cozy tub offers a calm refuge within this compact but well-appointed space.

Degrees of Separation

LARGE BATHROOMS BENEFIT from transition areas and compartmentalization. For example, a separate toilet enclosure with its own door within a larger bathroom makes the room comfortably usable by more than one person at a time. If there isn't room for a separate enclosure, a nook can often be planned that provides at least a semiprivate space for the toilet.

While tubs may look dramatic situated center stage in a room, many people feel uncomfortable and exposed when they're naked under the spotlight. It's better to situate a tub in an alcove or a corner. Dropping the ceiling over the tub is another way to help psychologically enclose the space and create a greater sense of intimacy. Degrees of separation such as these will help create the sense of privacy and refuge that make a bath comfortable and cozy.

▲ TRY TO IMAGINE this long and narrow room without a window; because of its light colors and plenty of natural light, this bathroom has a spacious and inviting feel. Here, a full-size walk-in shower alcove takes the place of the traditional tub, a practical substitution for those who prefer to shower rather than bathe.

▲ EVEN SMALL BATHROOMS can often be divided into more and less private areas. Try to locate the most intimate areas farthest from the entryway.

FIXTURE CLEARANCE GUIDELINES

When planning where to put fixtures, it's important to leave enough floor space around and in front of them. Follow these NKBA-recommended guidelines to ensure that there is adequate maneuvering room in your bathroom for people both with and without disabilities.

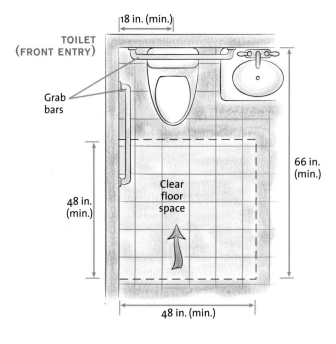

TOILET
(FRONT ENTRY)

18 in. (min.)

Grab bars

66 in. (min.)

Clear floor space

48 in. (min.)

48 in. (min.)

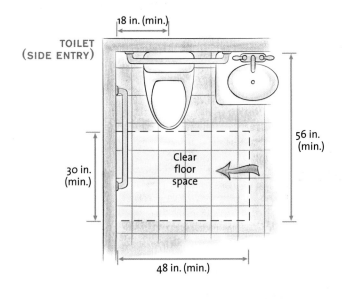

TOILET
(SIDE ENTRY)

18 in. (min.)

56 in. (min.)

30 in. (min.)

Clear floor space

48 in. (min.)

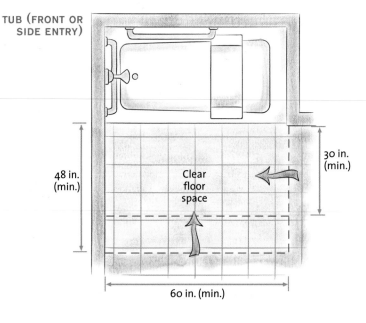

TUB (FRONT OR SIDE ENTRY)

30 in. (min.)

48 in. (min.)

Clear floor space

60 in. (min.)

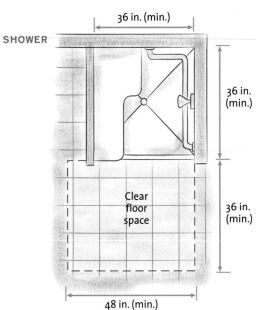

SHOWER

36 in. (min.)

36 in. (min.)

36 in. (min.)

Clear floor space

48 in. (min.)

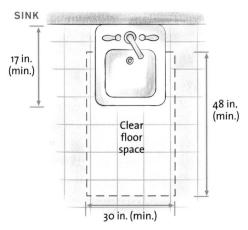

SINK

17 in. (min.)

48 in. (min.)

Clear floor space

30 in. (min.)

◄ADOPTING A EUROPEAN approach to bathroom design, this vanity area is open to the hallway and flanked by two separate compartments. Shown here is the bathing area, while the toilet is located in its own space to the left of the sink.

Organizing the Space

A common impulse in designing (or redesigning) a bathroom is to try to shoehorn fixtures into an already cramped space. If you've ever used a bathroom where this impulse was acted on unchecked (a toilet placed in a too-small location with inadequate clearance on either side, for example) then you know this is a mistake. Quite simply, bathroom fixtures each need a certain amount of floor space in order to be used properly.

Fortunately, plenty of ergonomic studies over the years have resulted in some clear fixture-clearance guidelines (see the drawing on the facing page). In general, toilets and sinks each occupy about 12 sq. ft. of floor space at a minimum, while a standard 5-ft. tub occupies about 30 sq. ft. (about 15 sq. ft. for the fixture itself and another 15 sq. ft. for clearance in front of the tub). As you arrange your bathroom's layout, use the clearance guidelines to make sure that each fixture is comfortable and safe.

▲ INSTEAD OF THE TRADITIONAL BATH/SHOWER combination, a compromise that usually results in less-than-satisfying baths and cramped and dangerous showers, this compact guest bath has a spacious walk-in shower instead. The glass partition next to the shower door lets more natural light into the interior of the room and helps connect the two spaces, making both feel larger.

Making a Small Bath Larger

WHILE THERE ARE WAYS to make a small room feel larger, sometimes the only recourse for a cramped space is to actually make it larger. In this bathroom remodel, a closet in an adjacent study was annexed to add more floor space, allowing more room to re-arrange the fixtures and add a larger window. At 7 ft. by 7 ft., this is still a modestly sized room that benefits from some space-enhancing strategies, such as a large mirror, a minimal tempered-glass partition between the tub and the vanity area, and plenty of natural light from both the new window and the sandblasted-glass entry door.

▲ A CLASSIC WAY TO MAKE A SMALL BATHROOM feel larger is by adding a large mirror. A pedestal sink adds to the illusion of space because it occupies such a small footprint, while the flanking vertical-grain Douglas fir cabinets provide plenty of much-needed storage.

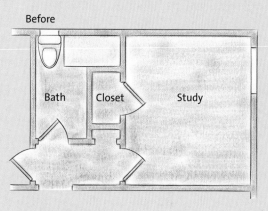

Before

Bath   Closet   Study

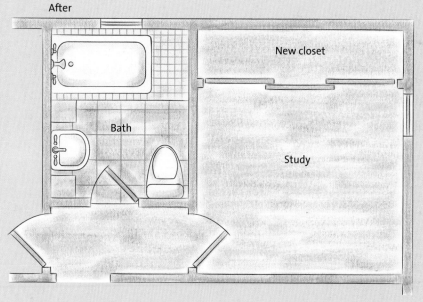

After

New closet

Bath

Study

Enlarging a tiny bath by moving walls and changing fixture locations isn't the cheapest option, but in some cases it is the only realistic alternative for creating a functional and attractive bathroom. Relocating the study closet allowed the original bathroom's cramped and dark L-shaped footprint to grow to 7 ft. x 7 ft., providing more room for the relocated fixtures, while a new and larger window centered in the wall above the tub helps flood the room with light.

Elements of Good Design

While using space efficiently is one important component in the planning process, a good bathroom design just looks *right*. Like any type of artistic expression, a bathroom's composition—good or bad—is the result of how the various individual elements work together. The key is to unite everything together in a way that looks logical, balanced, organized, and interesting.

Interior designers use basic design elements—*line, shape, space, form, texture,* and *color*—in order to achieve different looks. For example, vertical lines that carry the eye upward emphasize the height of a room and tend to lend a formal quality. Horizontal lines, on the other hand, widen a space; they lend a more relaxed feel to a room. Curved lines have a feminine quality and are particularly useful in softening the typically hard surfaces and rigid geometry found in a bathroom, while diagonal lines are dramatic.

As the parts of your bathroom begin to come together, pay attention to the interaction of these elements of design and use them to your advantage to get the right visual and emotional impact.

◄▲ ONE WAY TO HELP A SMALLER BATHROOM feel larger is to unify the design by repeating some of the individual design elements. In this bathroom, the keyhole-arch motif found in the mirrored medicine cabinet (above) is echoed by the arched tub alcove and by the end-wall details on the tub-surround (left).

Visual Space

▲ LIKE A CHAIR RAIL, this countertop's tile backsplash extends around the room. Besides adding visual interest, the strong horizontal component helps make the room feel larger.

THE ACTUAL PHYSICAL SIZE of a room (its shape) can be enhanced by the skillful use of placement, texture, pattern, and color, making its apparent size (its form) feel either larger or smaller. Here are a few simple ways to make a small room feel larger:

• Keep walls and floors a light color. Reducing or eliminating contrast (for example, by avoiding bright or dark-colored fixtures next to white walls) enhances the perception of space.

• Use patterns made up of small elements (small tiles, for example), which give the impression of being farther away.

• Keep vertical lines to a minimum and emphasize horizontal lines (vanity tops, shelving, and cabinets) which tend to visually expand the space.

• Use mirrors to transform structural barriers into reflective surfaces. Mirrors placed along one or two long walls will widen a narrow room.

• Repeating design elements—color, pattern, texture, size—makes a space feel more unified, and therefore larger.

▲ THOUGH SMALL, THIS BATHROOM DOESN'T FEEL CRAMPED due to the strong horizontal lines created by the dark blue accent tiles, which help draw the eye around the room.

▲IN A LARGE BATHROOM like this, different design strategies, such as the arched entry over the shower and the smaller arch in the tub alcove, can be used to help unify the space. Also, the subtle gradations of color in the travertine floor and wall tiles and granite countertops work with the faux finish on the wall to create a unified composition.

▶A STUDY IN SURFACES and textures, this bath contrasts cool stone and warm wood in a decidedly masculine-looking way. The stylized and deliberate orientation of the grain pattern on the wood cabinetry is a playful repetition of the diagonally patterned floor tile.

Choosing Colors and Textures

THE INTIMATE RED GLOW of a sunset; the cozy feeling of flannel sheets; smooth as silk; cool blue. More than just words, colors and textures suggest ideas that have an emotional impact. Here are a few guidelines to help you evoke specific moods in your bathroom using color and texture.

When we think of texture, we first think of touching something: a rough piece of bark, a smooth stone, a soft cotton towel. But texture also involves a visual response and memory, and this effect can be used in several different ways. For example, texture can be used to suggest different characteristics, such as masculinity (hard surfaces) or femininity (soft surfaces), simplicity (irregular and dull finishes), or refinement (even or shiny surfaces).

Color is often the most memorable feature of an interior design, and our psychological reactions to it are linked to primitive associations with nature. Red, like fire, can suggest danger and is exciting. Blue, like ice, is mysterious and suggests calm. Yellow, like sunshine, is cheerful. Green is associated with plants and grass and is peaceful and mellow. Brown tones suggest our connection to the earth (see the top photo). In general, colors on the red side of the spectrum are thought to be warm, while colors on the blue side of the spectrum are thought to

be cool. Colors toward the middle, like green, are considered neutral.

Remember that colors are seen truly only in natural daylight, so artificial lighting has an effect on color as well, both by having its own color temperature (see Chapter 6) and by its intensity (dim light tends to neutralize color).

◄ THE REDDISH-BROWN TONES of the wood ceiling and tile floor in this bathroom help warm up the space and complement the neutral colors of the walls and fixtures.

▼ THE RICH COLORS and informal look of the unfitted furniture in this bathroom combine with the rough texture of the room's timber-frame construction to give the room a peaceful and rustic simplicity.

Bathroom Safety Tips

MORE THAN A QUARTER **of all home accidents occur in the bathroom. The most frequent mishap? Slipping and falling while getting into or out of the tub. Here are some commonsense tips for making your bathroom safer:**

- **Install grab bars in potentially slippery spots.**
- **Use slip-resistant materials and surfaces in wet areas.**
- **Use temperature-regulating tub and shower valves.**
- **Install locks on medicine cabinets.**
- **Be sure bathroom outlets are protected by GFCI (ground-fault circuit interrupter) circuitry.**
- **Install only privacy locks on bathroom doors, which can be quickly and easily opened in case of emergency.**

▲ WITH DOUBLE GLASS DOORS, a curbless threshold, and sturdy yet stylish grab bars, this shower is fully wheelchair-accessible. Note the built-in bench to the left as you enter the shower.

Accessibility & Safety

It goes without saying that bathroom safety should be paramount in any good bathroom design. Unfortunately, common sense is sometimes clouded by our aesthetic sense. Who doesn't admire the gleaming surface of a shiny marble floor? But a floor like this is slippery when wet, and bathrooms are often quite wet. In fact, the bathroom is one of the most dangerous areas in the home. Fortunately, a little planning goes a long way in reducing the risks in a bathroom.

Accessibility is also an important consideration in all aspects of home design. The built environment is geared primarily toward adults in perfect health, which ac-counts for less than a quarter of the population. For the remaining 75 percent, size and physical limitations sometimes make it difficult—if not impossible—to use the facilities that adults take for granted.

While people can adapt to their environment to some extent, a better and safer approach is to adapt the environment to meet the changing needs of those using it. Accessibility doesn't necessarily require extensive modifications or expensive fixtures or accessories, and in most cases it can be enhanced with very little impact on the overall appearance of the bath.

▲INSTEAD OF A SEPARATE SHOWER ENCLOSURE, this universally accessible bathroom features an open design and a waterproof floor. The vanity is also designed to be fully accessible, with an open area underneath for wheelchair access and lever-handle faucets.

▲THIS BATHROOM IS DESIGNED for easy access, with a pocket door that slides out of sight when not in use, separating the bathroom from the adjoining bedroom, and an open custom-built vanity. The spacious, door-less shower on the far side of the vanity has plenty of maneuvering room and a large window for adequate natural light.

Making a Bathroom Accessible

MOST BATHROOMS CAN BE MODIFIED to make them more accessible for users of all ages and with a wide range of physical abilities:

- Install grab bars in strategic locations, such as tubs and showers. Make sure the grab bars are fastened securely.
- Use lever handles for doors and fixtures rather than round knobs, which are more difficult to grasp.
- Follow minimum fixture clearance guidelines (see p. 24).
- Provide generously sized passageways and doorways.
- Avoid thresholds in doorways and other changes in floor-surface elevations.
- Locate tub and shower controls so they can be operated from a seated position and from both inside and outside the unit.
- Locate switches, outlets, and other controls so they can be operated by someone in a seated position.
- Provide seating in both shower and tub areas.
- Provide a hand-held shower in place of (or in addition to) a fixed showerhead.
- Consider a sink design that offers knee space below the sink.

- Use tilting mirrors or full-height mirrors, or make sure that mirrors extend all the way down to sink level.
- Provide easily accessible storage (both drawers and cabinetry) between 15 in. and 48 in. off the floor.

In order to be accessible for those confined to wheelchairs, a bathroom needs to have adequate clearance in front of fixtures, a wide doorway for entry and exit, open knee space under the sink, a seating/transfer area adjacent to the tub, and strategically placed grab bars for safety.

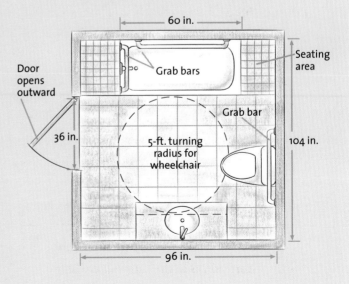

Finishing the Bath in Style

L IBERAL OR CONSERVATIVE? That's a question you'll have to answer as you sort out bathroom styles, materials, and finishes. Do your tastes run toward the classic or the eclectic? Are you more comfortable in a bathroom filled with gleaming white fixtures and hygienic tiled floors, or is there a radical element in you calling out for more color, more pizzazz, something, well, different?

Vintage or contemporary, the style you choose and the fixtures and finishes you select go hand in hand. Tile, of course, remains an ever-popular favorite for all styles of bathrooms thanks to its versatility. But you might also want to consider the organic appeal of natural stone, which rivals tile in its durability and affordability. Metal and glass both have a number of applications in a bathroom and can lend it a modern, industrial quality. And, of course, there are synthetic finishes—like colorful plastic laminates and tough solid surfacing materials—that can be used in any number of ways to spice up your bathroom. In fact, there's a whole palette of beautiful and durable natural and synthetic finish materials available to choose from. To help your bathroom take shape, refer to the following pages for examples of style and substance.

◄ CERAMIC TILE, A POPULAR FINISH MATERIAL because of its durability and beauty, is used on the floor, countertop, and shower walls in this bright and cheerful bath. The shower also has a glass-block partition wall, which keeps water in its place without blocking out the natural light.

Selecting a Style

O FTEN A HOUSE'S ARCHITECTURAL STYLE plays a major role in determining the style of its bathrooms. For example, if your home has beautiful Craftsman-style detailing, it makes sense to incorporate those same features in your bathroom's design. But other houses are less bound by tradition, and the bathrooms in them offer a wider range of options for self-expression. Whether you remain contemporary or try to re-create a period look, choose a style that reflects your own interests, that creates an atmosphere that invigorates you in the morning and relaxes you at night, and that makes the room a desirable place to be.

▲ WHITE SUBWAY-TILE WAIN-SCOTING, small hexagonal floor tiles, and Anaglypta™, a textured, linoleum-based, paintable wall covering, were typical details used in 1920s-era bathrooms.

◄ A BLEND OF the traditional and the contemporary, this seaside master bathroom and the home that it's located in were inspired by the surrounding Shingle-style homes built along Maine's coast at the end of the 19th century. The bath takes advantage of the vista toward the nearby harbor with a big bay window in the tub area; the frameless glass shower enclosure is a decidedly modern touch.

▲ MANY CONTEMPORARY MASTER BATHS have an open floor plan and are incorporated into the adjacent living areas. This one features a custom-colored mosaic tile floor and tub deck, which provides a colorful contrast to the smooth texture and neutral tones of the massive limestone tile walls.

In the Japanese Tradition

INSPIRATION FOR A BATHROOM DESIGN can come from a particular culture just as easily as from a particular period of time or architectural style. In this Vermont mountainside retreat, the homeowners' interest in Japanese art and architecture is reflected in the first-floor bath, which is designed to resemble a traditional Japanese communal bath.

Complete with tatami mats, wooden buckets, and a stone and bamboo fountain, the bath also features a gorgeous tile mural (by Christine Merrimen), which is a copy of an 18th-century painting. Characteristic of the *sento* (a public bath), this room features an open layout and generous use of natural materials like slate, granite, and wood, creating an environment that invites contemplation and ritual.

▲ A TILE MURAL depicting an 18th-century Japanese painting contrasts with the darker granite scrubbing bench and slate floor in this bath.

◄TUCKED INTO THE ATTIC of a 1906 California bungalow, this renovated bathroom has a contemporary feel while paying homage to the home's Arts and Crafts character. A skylight in the shower (photo above right) provides additional headroom and floods the rest of the bathroom with more natural light. The polished nickel sink and fixtures and the wooden vanity top (inset photo, above left) were inspired by the butler's pantry in the nearby Gamble House, one of Charles and Henry Greene's classic Craftsman-style "Ultimate Bungalows," which was built in Pasadena in 1909. The countertop is made from goncolo alves, a tough, stain-resistant wood that is similar to teak in its appearance and resistance to rot.

▲PERIOD-STYLE FIXTURES, painted beadboard paneling, and a geometrically painted floor give this bathroom a turn-of-the-century informality.

◀A WOOD FLOOR AND AREA RUG add a warm contrast to the old-fashioned fixtures and white-painted wainscoting in this traditionally styled bath.

An Arts and Crafts Bath

I**N THIS BATH**, located in a 1919 Craftsman-style house in California, what began as a relatively minor ceiling repair blossomed into a major renovation with the discovery of old and deteriorated galvanized plumbing. The bad news was that the plumbing would need replacing, along with the tile floor and fixtures; the good news was that the bath could be improved by enlarging the shower, installing new fixtures, and redecorating so that it more truly represented its Craftsman heritage. Many details give this bathroom its Arts and Crafts flavor, including the custom-crafted quarter-sawn oak medicine cabinet and freestanding storage unit, a reproduction claw-foot soaking tub, and the intricately executed tile floor and wainscoting.

▲ A REPRODUCTION CLAW-FOOT TUB (left)complements the bath's style while mortise-and-tenon joinery, Mission styling, and quartersawn oak construction give this medicine cabinet its Arts and Crafts appeal.

In order to repair damage and bring the room's plumbing and electrical wiring up to code, this bathroom was gutted back to the wall studs and floor joists. But because the fixture locations worked efficiently, the basic layout of the room remained unchanged.

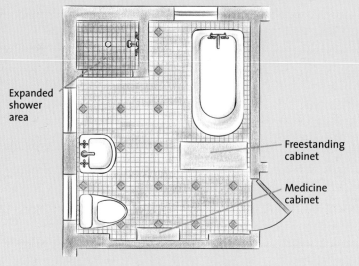

Expanded shower area

Freestanding cabinet

Medicine cabinet

▲ A CUSTOM-BUILT, MISSION-STYLE, quartersawn oak storage unit takes center stage in this renovated Arts and Crafts bathroom. New fixtures with traditional styling improve the bathroom's function, while Craftsman-type detailing—like the meticulously tiled floor and wainscot—help it retain its character and charm.

◀ THIS DROP-IN WHIRLPOOL TUB is a concession to modernity, but the tile floor, beadboard paneling, and bright white finish are timeless.

▲ THIS VERMONT BATHROOM utilizes salvaged fixtures and old-fashioned tile to give it a vintage look. The stub-foot tub is an original fixture to the house, while the sink was found at an architectural salvage yard.

◀ LOCATED IN A SHINGLE-STYLE HOUSE on Nantucket, this bath's white-painted beadboard paneling and oiled wood floor are details that might have been found aboard one of the island's 19th-century whaling ships.

▶ WITH A SIMPLE WOK SINK and *shoji*-style closet doors, this contemporary bath has an Asian influence. The countertop is made of black slate.

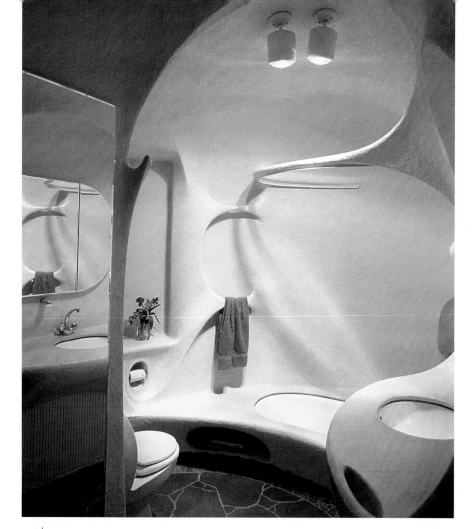

◄INSTEAD OF FLAT WALLS AND RIGHT ANGLES, this womblike master bath was sculpted using gunite, a sprayed-in-place type of concrete that is more commonly used to build swimming pools.

Upgrading a Basement Bathroom

Located in the bottom level of a suburban tract house, this clean and modern master bath renovation has a rich look, yet was built using relatively inexpensive materials. Stainless-steel columns and ceiling coving contrast with the natural warmth of travertine marble, 12x12 tiles on the walls and countertops, and ash veneer cabinetry.

A basement bathroom doesn't get a lot of natural light, so the indirect cove lighting and numerous recessed and surface-mounted fixtures play a big role in keeping this bathroom light and bright. Note too the glass-block detailing on the wall above the whirlpool tub, which allows what daylight there is to penetrate into the room while still maintaining privacy.

Located in a basement, this bathroom has plenty of room but not a lot of natural light. Dedicating smaller areas to specific functions, differentiating between them with stainless-steel columns and varied ceiling heights, and making sure each area has ample artificial light helps define the boundaries while unifying the large space.

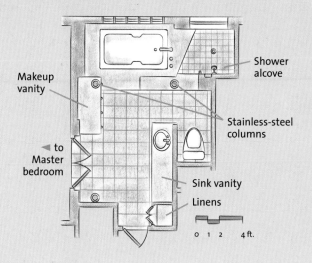

Makeup vanity

◄ to Master bedroom

Shower alcove

Stainless-steel columns

Sink vanity

Linens

0 1 2   4 ft.

►THIS MAHOGANY-VENEER VANITY is part of a spacious master bathroom that shares space with the adjoining bedroom. The vanity is topped with a glass countertop that is painted on the underside, providing depth and color to the countertop.

▲WHILE IT ALMOST LOOKS LIKE LEATHER, this rugged countertop is cast from concrete and treated with a chemical stain. Stained concrete in the shower area is embedded with washed pebbles.

►EXPOSED PLUMBING, surface-mounted wiring, and lots of concrete lend an industrial look to this loft bathroom. The shower wall, floor (which tilts toward a perimeter trough instead of a central drain), and countertop are carved from bluestone granite.

Room for Two

LOCATED IN AN OLD BRICK ROWHOUSE in Portland, Maine, this master bath features a central dressing room with floor-to-ceiling storage accessed by a custom-fabricated, aluminum library-type ladder. The toilet and shower area are contained in a separate "wet room," which is separated from the main bath by a sliding translucent glass door that provides privacy and keeps moisture under control by keeping splashes in their place. Note the cozy carpeting underfoot in the dressing area, a nice feature for Maine's cool mornings.

▲ THE POCKET DOOR TO THE TOILET AND SHOWER is made up of two layers of sandblasted glass facing inward, giving the door a translucent quality and keeping it easier to clean.

◄ THE CENTRAL DRESSING AREA has a high ceiling with floor-to-ceiling storage. It's well lit by a custom-fabricated ceiling fixture, strategically placed recessed lighting, and linear fluorescent lights diffused by sandblasted-glass shades.

Natural Finish Materials

In a bathroom, style and substance go hand in hand. While design plays a significant role in a bathroom's overall feel, material selection also informs its sense of style, and the same type of materials can be used in different ways to create different effects. Tile and stone, for instance, are classic bathroom materials that are versatile enough to be used in a wide range of period and contemporary baths. Metal, glass, and concrete, on the other hand, have an industrial quality that seems most at home in a contemporary setting. If you're looking to introduce an element of warmth into any type of bathroom, don't forget about wood, a perfect counterpoint to the colder and harder materials that are usually found there.

◀▲ THE RICH, UNEVEN TEXTURE of these handmade tiles give this bathroom a rustic, Southwestern touch and are a good match for the rough plastered walls and dark wood trim. The glass block built into the partition wall lets natural light into the relatively small shower enclosure, helping to keep it from feeling too confined.

▲ SLATE, GLASS, and small ceramic-tile accents are among the palette of materials used in this beautiful contemporary bathroom. Cleft slate has a rough surface texture, a feature accentuated by the irregularly cut upper edge of the stone.

◄ THIS COLOR-INTENSIVE BATHTUB is covered with handmade Mexican tiles, giving the tub a festive and irregular texture that's inviting to both the hand and the eye.

▲NATURAL STONE'S WIDE RANGE
OF SIZES, textures, and colors can
be mixed and matched for a number of different looks. Here, for example, the small tumbled-stone
mosaics are a good choice because
they easily follow the curve of the
tub deck and create a pleasing
contrast with its green stone slab
as well as with the smoother polished surfaces of the stone tiles
used for the floor and walls.

▶BATH TIME BECOMES A
CARIBBEAN VACATION with the
help of this bold ceramic mosaic
design. Ceramic artist Pat
Wehrman, who refers to tile
glazes as her "box of crayons,"
uses layered and subtle colors
and her knowledge of marine
biology to create her colorful
seascapes.

A Stone Bath

WHILE NATURAL STONE'S BEAUTY **and** durability make it a good choice for any bathroom, too much of a good thing can lead to bathrooms that feel cold and clinical. Not so with this bath, despite the green slate used on both the floors and the walls. For one thing, the slate itself has a textured surface, variegated patterns, and veins of color in it, all of which tend to soften its presence. In addition, the room's gently curved white plaster cornice and curved skylight wells draw the eye upward, help flood the room with light, and soften the rigid geometry of the slate tiles.

This kind of bathroom requires a meticulous tile layout to minimize the use of cut tiles and unnecessary grout lines, and it feels spacious and uncluttered thanks to the floating mirror located behind the floating sandstone countertop and the spare shower enclosure.

▲THIS SANDSTONE COUNTERTOP with hammered copper sinks appears to be floating in a sea of green slate. The floor-to-ceiling mirror behind the countertop reflects light from the sculpted skylight above, flooding the room with natural light.

◄THE SHOWER ENCLOSURE is made of tempered-glass panels, which are held in place by glass channels hidden in the grout lines.

▶ SLATE HAS A RICH, ORGANIC LOOK and is available in various colors and surface finishes. The cleft slate shown here has a rougher texture that provides good traction for floors and walls, but because slate is soft and somewhat porous, it needs to be sealed and properly maintained to prevent staining.

Choosing Tile

I F YOU'RE CONSIDERING TILE for your bathroom, you'll find an enormous variety of styles, colors, types, and price points to choose from. Where do you begin? First of all, consider what the tile will be used for. For example, floor tiles need to be durable and slip resistant, while wall tiles don't. Relatively hard tiles that rate at least 6 or 7 on the Mohs scale (a 1-to-10 scale used by tile manufacturers to indicate the hardness or softness of a tile) and that have a textured or matte glaze are best underfoot.

Ease of cleaning is an important consideration for tiles intended for bath or shower walls; a shiny glaze is better for these applications, while hardness is less of an issue. To simplify the process, choose a few samples that you like, take them home, and put them through a few scratching, rubbing, and scuffing tests to approximate the kind of use that they might expect to encounter in your bathroom.

▶ WHEN CHOOSING BATHROOM TILE, consider where it will be used as well as how it fits with the bathroom's overall design.

◀ THIS BATHROOM IS NEARLY 18 FT. LONG and looks out over the ocean. The countertop and tub deck are made from polished limestone, while the floor is tiled with tumbled-marble mosaics, which have a rougher texture that provides better footing.

▼ MARBLE IS A BEAUTIFUL and popular bathroom finish material, but is generally also the most susceptible to staining among the natural stones (as shown here). Highly polished marbles are most vulnerable, and like most stones, marble needs to be sealed with a penetrating silicone sealer that is maintained regularly.

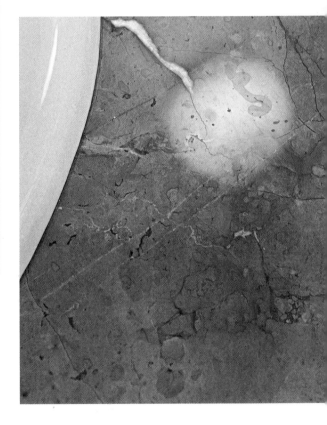

◀ NATURAL STONES LIKE GRANITE (top), soapstone (center), and slate (bottom) are popular finish materials for bathrooms (prefabricated granite bathroom countertops are even available at some home centers) because of their natural beauty and durability. Stone is available in both highly polished and matte (or honed) finishes.

▲ THE RICH BROWN-RED COLOR of this frame-and-panel mahogany-wood apron warms up this bathroom, and because the left panel is secured by screws, it provides easy access to the pump of this whirlpool tub.

▶ THIS TUB IS STRICTLY for soaking, so errant splashes and spills that might otherwise cause damage can be quickly mopped up here. This random-width pine floor has the beautiful patina that characterizes an antique wood floor.

Why Not Wood?

WOOD HAS A NATURAL WARMTH **and texture** that makes it a good choice for countering the sometimes clinical appearance of other bathroom finish materials. What's not so good is wood's susceptibility to moisture damage, but given proper preparation and protection, most wood species can be used in the bathroom.

For example, wood floors with a protective coating-type finish are a nice touch underfoot, particularly in bathrooms that don't see a lot of boisterous water play. Wood paneling, such as wainscot, is also a great choice for covering walls and ceilings. Wood can even be used for countertops; naturally decay-resistant woods like teak, redwood, or mahogany are good choices here, but even properly prepped and finished maple butcher block will work.

▲ THIS PAINTED MAPLE CABINET is topped by a countertop of longleaf pine.

▲ FOR THE WET AREAS in this bathroom, a cast concrete countertop and Chinese slate tiles were used. The rest of the bath employs panels of medium-density fiberboard veneered with anigre, a wood with a subtle grain pattern and warm, caramel color.

◄ A POCKET ENTRY DOOR with a frosted-glass panel lets in light from the hallway, while artificial lighting hidden above the false ceiling illuminates the top of the anigre-paneled walls.

▲SUPPORTED BY A **custom-fabricated** stainless-steel column, this crackled-glass countertop draws a thin line across this contemporary bathroom. The sink drain is incorporated into the column, while the water-supply lines for the faucet are hidden in the wall.

▲HAND-CUT, STAINLESS-STEEL TILES with beveled sides and a brushed finish line the floor, walls, and ceiling of this ultrasleek industrial bathroom. The shower floor has removable stainless-steel grating for traction and cleaning.

◄A STARTLING BLUE COUNTERTOP painted with automotive lacquer supports this custom-fabricated stainless-steel vanity. A porcelain sink with a metallic-glazed finish matches the imported tiles on the floor and walls.

Stainless Steel

BESIDES ITS GOOD LOOKS, **stainless steel is** tough, rust resistant, easy to clean, and sanitary. A nickel-rich alloy of chrome and iron first invented in 1913 by a British metallurgist looking to improve gun barrels, stainless steel has found its way into sinks, faucets, panels, and even floor and wall tiles. It's available in a range of thicknesses and surface textures that can help hide scratches and fingerprints.

▲ WHILE COUNTERTOPS AND BATHROOM SINKS can be made of other metals, such as copper and zinc, stainless steel is the most commonly used metal. It's nonporous and nonstaining, easy to clean, and requires much less maintenance than other metals. The brushed finish shown here hides fingerprints better than more highly polished finishes.

▲ LIKE A POOL OF WATER, this glass sink is surrounded by iridescent glass mosaic tiles. Light entering the room from the skylight above is refracted and reflected by the glass surfaces, filling the small room with depth and color.

◀ COPPER IS A BEAUTIFUL, easily fabricated soft metal that is most often used for roofs, chimney flashing, and plumbing. Here, sheets of copper have been bent and soldered into countertops, while a length of copper plumbing pipe and some common fittings have been transformed into a towel bar.

CONCRETE

▲ ONE OF THE ADVANTAGES OF CONCRETE is the ability to cast it into sculptural forms, like this curving slab countertop. Extending the faucet handle out the side rather than the top adds another unique detail to this highly stylized bathroom.

▲ THOUGH THE SINKS AND TUB ARE DARK, this bathroom feels warm and bright thanks to the large mirrors, plentiful natural light, and fir cabinetry. The fixtures are built of Syndecrete™, a composite of cement, recycled materials, and industrial by-products with half the weight of regular concrete and twice the compressive strength.

▶UNEXPECTEDLY, JEWEL-LIKE GLASS BEADS glitter from the surface of this dark blue concrete countertop, a delicate and colorful contradiction to concrete's more familiar role as a basic construction material used for foundations and sidewalks.

Rock Solid

ONCRETE IS A FAMILIAR AND VERSATILE **building material that has moved out of the basement and into the kitchens and bathrooms of many homes. Strong and economical, it lends itself to a variety of applications, including familiar precast blocks that can be used to build both straight and curving walls.**

Concrete can also be cast into countertops, allowing designers and builders to take advantage of its sculptural qualities. While one thinks of concrete as having a coarse texture and drab coloring, it can actually be given a satin-smooth finish and treated with a variety of pigments. It also makes an industrial-strength flooring for both inside and outside the bath.

◀A CURVING WALL built from plastered concrete block and glass block separates these two bathrooms. Oak leaves cut from 12-ga. copper sheet embellish the poured concrete floor of the near bath, while exposed pebbles dot the floor of the far bath.

◀WITH INDUSTRIAL-GRADE concrete walls and floor and welded iron fittings, this bathroom looks more like it belongs in a warehouse than in a residential setting. The cast concrete tub is sealed with epoxy pool paint.

Synthetic Materials

OLID-SURFACE MATERIALS, such as DuPont's Corian®, are ideal for bathroom countertops because of their water and stain resistance, durability, and ability to be fabricated almost like wood. Composite materials made from ground-up minerals like quartz with a resin binder are a variation on this theme. Of course, there's still that familiar standby, high-pressure plastic laminate—think Formica®—which is a less-expensive alternative that offers a wide range of design options. Laminates are available in an incredible variety of colors and textures, and you'll find them on floors and walls as well as countertops. Finally, don't forget about the decorative potential of the right paint or wallpaper, perhaps the most cost-effective and dramatic means of transforming a humdrum bathroom into a showcase.

▲ WHILE SOLID-SURFACE MATERIALS can be manufactured to look like stone, they're also available in solid colors, like this striking black countertop.

◄ THIS COUNTERTOP IS MADE FROM CAESARSTONE™, a quartz composite material manufactured in Israel, and is complemented with a tumbled-stone and glass-tile backsplash. Harder, less porous, and more stain resistant than granite, quartz composites are often chosen because of their quiet and consistent color and texture, as opposed to the less-predictable appearance of natural stone.

◄ PART OF THE APPEAL of solid-surface materials is that they can be fabricated almost as easily as wood. This countertop features a sculpted edge treatment and an integral solid-surface bowl that's been seamlessly attached to the countertop, making it very easy to keep clean.

Counter Options

THERE'S A WIDE RANGE of durable and water-resistant manmade and natural finish materials that can be used for bathroom countertops (and for floors and walls as well). Because bathroom countertops aren't typically very expansive, they don't take as big of a bite out of the budget as kitchen countertops do. Still, it's useful to have a frame of reference when trying to determine which countertop material to use in your bathroom. Here's a brief comparison of the popular countertop materials, keeping in mind that cost estimates are for rough comparison only.

MATERIAL	PROS	CONS	COST (APPROX., INSTALLED PER SQ.FT.)
Laminates	Vast array of colors and styles	More susceptible to scratches	$5 to $15
Solid-surface and composite materials	Nonstaining, repairable	Expensive, can scorch	$50 to $100
Ceramic tile	Durable surface, wide variety of colors, textures, and sizes	Grout can stain, irregular surface	$30 and up; varies widely depending on type of tile and installation
Stone (granite, marble, limestone, slate, soapstone, travertine, etc.)	Durable, heat resistant, range of colors and textures	Can stain, expensive	$50 to $100+
Butcher block (and other woods)	User-friendly surface	Can stain, mildew, and rot	$30 to $85
Stainless steel (and other metals)	Nonstaining, easy to clean, heat resistant	Can dent and develop scratches	$80 to $100
Concrete	Durable, heat resistant, can be cast into a variety of shapes	Can fade, stain, and discolor, as well as crack	$60 to $100

COMPOSITES & SOLID-SURFACE MATERIALS

▲▲ A NEW ALTERNATIVE TO SOLID-SURFACE MATERIALS are composites, such as Silestone™ (left), Trespa™ (second from left), and Zodiaq™ (third from left). Silestone and Zodiaq are blends of quartz, resin binders, and pigments that are nonporous, nonstaining, and heat and scratch resistant, while Trespa is a lower-cost resin composite that is essentially a superthick plastic laminate. Fireslate2 and other fiber cement products (right) are cement-based composites that are strong and heat resistant, as well as relatively inexpensive compared to solid-surfacing.

▲ SOLID-SURFACE COUNTERTOPS such as this one are usually fabricated from two layers along the edge to give the counter more visual weight. Though subtle, the seam is usually visible on closer inspection, though it generally doesn't detract from the overall appeal of the countertop.

▶ A CONTRASTING INLAID EDGE TREATMENT is one of the design possibilities available with a solid-surface countertop. This one also has an integral—though contrasting—sink.

◄ FABRICATED OUT OF A SINGLE THICKNESS of solid-surface material, this countertop's thin profile facilitates the transition to the winglike shelves on either side of the vanity.

Solid-Surface Materials

DuPONT BEGAN THE SOLID-SURFACE REVOLUTION when it developed a technique for blending natural minerals with acrylic resin. Now, along with DuPont's popular Corian, there are several other solid-surface materials to choose from, including Formica's Surell® and Wilsonart's Gibraltar®. While each has different compositions, colors, and textures, all solid-surface materials share certain qualities and characteristics that make them ideal for a bathroom environment.

Unlike plastic laminates, solid-surface materials can be repaired if they get burned or scratched simply by sanding and buffing out the defect. Nonporous and easy to clean, solid-surfacing is unaffected by most chemicals (with the exception of some paint removers and oven cleaners), and is fairly resistant to heat as well.

Most manufacturers make their solid-surface materials available in ¼-in., ½-in., and ¾-in. thicknesses of varying lengths and widths. While they're most often used to fabricate countertops, their smooth, easily cleaned surfaces make them ideal for tub and shower surrounds. Some manufacturers offer thinner ⅛-in.-thick veneers for this purpose.

Premolded solid-surface sinks are available in a limited number of sizes, shapes, and colors to coordinate with most manufacturers' product lines. Specialty shops can fabricate custom countertops with seamlessly welded integral sinks that match (or contrast with) your chosen countertop material.

The best way to find the solid-surface material that is right for your bathroom is to get sample kits containing small blocks of the actual material from each manufacturer. That way, you can accurately compare the colors and textures that each has to offer.

▲ SOLID-SURFACE MATERIALS like Corian (top), Avonite™ (center), and Surell (bottom) are nonstaining, easy to clean, durable, and can be fabricated into countertops with integral sinks.

▶ ▲ THIS LONG, CUSTOM-BUILT
maple and cherry vanity cabinet is
topped with a laminate countertop that features a maple edge
treatment with a cherry inlay
(right). Note how the sliding vanity
doors mimic the *shoji*-style sliding
translucent screens at the entry to
the narrow bath (above). Instead
of traditional rice paper, these *shoji*
screens are made with water-
resistant acrylic-modified paper,
which is far more durable and
practical in a bathroom.

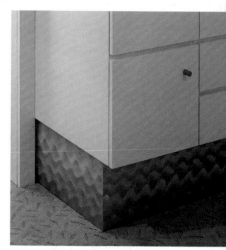

▲THIS VANITY CABINET'S TOEKICK
has been wrapped with a decorative plastic laminate that has a
metallic brushed-aluminum finish.

▲THIS COUNTERTOP HAS BEEN FABRICATED with a color-core plastic laminate, which virtually eliminates the seam typically found at the edges of
standard laminate.

All About Plastic Laminate

First introduced in 1927, Formica and other brands of plastic laminate remain the most popular kitchen and bathroom countertop material. Understandably so: Plastic laminate is available in a staggering variety of colors and textures, is relatively easily fabricated into countertops, and at around $1 to $4 per sq. ft. (for uninstalled sheet goods), it's a bargain. Plastic laminate is made of several layers of different types of paper that are sandwiched together and saturated with phenolic resin, then cooked under high pressure until the ingredients bond together into a single sheet of plastic.

In addition to the familiar varieties of laminate, there are some interesting recent variations. One of these is solid-core laminate; because it doesn't have a kraft paper core, it doesn't have the corresponding dark line at the edge like regular laminate, and corners can be fabricated that look almost seamless. There are also decorative metal laminates, which have almost mirrorlike bronze, gold, copper, brass, and aluminum finishes. You can't use these for countertops, but they can be used for some interesting cabinetry designs.

Because plastic laminate isn't indestructible, choose the color and finish with care if you plan on using it in a high-wear application. For example, matte finishes are better at hiding scratches than glossy finishes, while textured finishes are hard to keep clean. Darker laminate colors also seem to highlight every speck of dust or errant glob of toothpaste, as well as scratches.

▲ A SANDWICH OF KRAFT PAPER impregnated with phenolic resin and topped with a decorative layer of melamine-protected paper, high-pressure plastic laminate is available in dozens of colors and patterns.

▶ COMBINING THE WARMTH OF WOOD with the practicality of plastic laminate, Formica's Ligna™ wood surfacing is a sandwich of real wood veneers laminated to a phenolic resin core. The consistent finish and ease of application make it a good choice for creating unique bathroom cabinetry designs.

◄LAMINATES AREN'T JUST FOUND on countertops anymore. Increasingly popular as a floor finish in other rooms of the house, some manufacturers warrant their laminate flooring, which can be manufactured to look like virtually any type of finish, for use in bathrooms and other potentially wet areas as well.

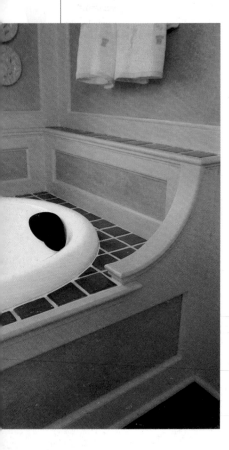

▶ ▲ INSPIRED BY A PHOTO of Monet's summer home, the blues and greens of this Rhode Island waterfront cottage reflect the colors found in the water and foliage around the house. On the ceiling, painted bed molding applied to the vertical-grain fir paneling creates a coffered look (right), while the tub is trimmed out like a sleigh and finished to match the rest of the bathroom (above).

◀UNCONTROLLED HUMIDITY is problematic in any bathroom, but is particularly troublesome if there are any wall coverings. Unlike a shower, however, this soaking tub doesn't generate much humidity, although an adequate ventilation system is still important for any type of bathroom, regardless of the type of finish used on the floors, walls, and ceilings.

▲UNIFORM GREEN WALLS make a good background for the heart-pine countertop and naturally finished vanity in this cheerful children's bathroom.

◀THIS GUEST BATHROOM'S bold wallpaper design was chosen to match the printed checkerboard pattern on the tiled countertop and the reds and greens used to decorate the adjoining bedroom. The ceiling is papered with wall covering that has a textured pattern.

Bathtubs and Showers

We use soap and water to get clean, but bathing and showering is about more than simple hygiene. When we begin the day with an invigorating shower, we jump-start our body and mind for the busy day ahead. At the end of the day, or during weekends or vacations when the pace of life isn't quite so hectic, a long soak in a hot bath relaxes the body and calms the mind.

Standard 5-ft. bathtubs fitted with a combination bath/shower valve and either a shower curtain or glass shower doors have long been providing yeoman's service in all types of bathrooms. But there are a lot more choices now. Why not a whirlpool? How about two (or more) showerheads or a hand-held shower? What about multiple body-jets to turn an ordinary shower into a vertical spa? How about built-in seating or room for two? And why not a separate bath and shower?

Of course, your options will be determined in part by your bathroom's size, purpose, and budget, but even the most basic of bathrooms will benefit from a little creative thinking. Whether your bathroom and budget are large or small, there are dozens of wonderful ways to get into hot water; here's a look at some of the possibilities.

◄ SPACIOUS AND INVITING, this beautiful master bath features a spa-like soaking tub for relaxing and a separate shower area with a frameless glass enclosure for getting clean. The tub deck extends into the shower, a feature that provides generous seating in the shower and helps to visually unify the two areas. The transom windows in the shower area are another nice touch, keeping the space light, bright, and private.

Bathing Spaces

A LITTLE OVER A CENTURY AGO, a Wisconsin farm-implement manufacturer named John Kohler began sprinkling white enamel powder on his cast-iron horse troughs, baking them, and welding legs on them to create the first residential bathtubs. In some ways, not much has changed since then, because hefty claw-foot tubs—in both retro and contemporary styles—are just as popular as ever. But tubs have evolved too, taking advantage of new materials and technologies; now they're available in almost every size, shape, and color. From simple soaking tubs to therapeutic whirlpools to perhaps even an indoor exercise pool, there is a style to fit every taste and budget, no matter how simple or extravagant.

▲WITH COMFORTABLE CURVES, heavy mass to retain heat, and a durable porcelain-enamel finish that makes them easy to keep clean, cast-iron tubs are ideal for soaking. This one has a shower ring and curtain for those mornings when time is at a premium.

◄THIS INTIMATE SOAKING TUB is tucked into its own private, light-filled alcove. The wide surround provides room for decorative objects, as well as bathing necessities.

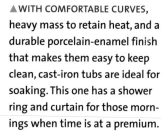

◀STEPS OF SPANISH TILE lead up to an oval whirlpool tub, a favorite place in this hilltop house because of the terrific views of the valley below and the hills in the distance. Floral silk shades and a vanity chair upholstered with terry cloth give this master bathroom a feminine touch.

The Japanese Bath

THE JAPANESE HAVE LONG UNDERSTOOD that a good bath is about more than good hygiene. Whether done at a *sento* (a public bath) or in an *ofuro* (the soaking tub found in most residences), the Japanese ritual of rinsing, washing, and soaking can give bath time a tranquil—if not spiritual—quality.

Japanese soaking tubs are smaller but deeper than their American counterparts and often are equipped with seats. This makes them good for soaking, because you can immerse yourself up to your shoulders easily, but not so good for washing. Washing and rinsing are done before you enter the bath; the tub is strictly for relaxation and contemplation. After finishing a bath, the tub is left full of water for the next family member to enjoy.

▲JAPANESE SOAKING TUBS, or *ofuro*, are smaller and deeper than American tubs, making it easier to totally immerse oneself in hot water. They're a good alternative to the popular but often unused whirlpools that are found in many master bath suites.

▲ROUGE TOILE DRAPERY PANELS in this young girl's bathroom pull back to reveal a romantic slipper-style cast-iron lion's paw tub.

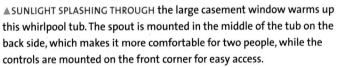

▲SUNLIGHT SPLASHING THROUGH the large casement window warms up this whirlpool tub. The spout is mounted in the middle of the tub on the back side, which makes it more comfortable for two people, while the controls are mounted on the front corner for easy access.

▶SALTILLO FLOOR TILES and a slate tub deck provide textural contrast to the arches, mullions, and wainscoting in this expansive master bath. There's an enclosed glass shower stall just to the left of the bath.

◄IT LOOKS LIKE A CLASSIC, but this is a reproduction cast-iron claw-foot tub nestled into the corner of this spare bathroom. While not totally waterproof, the ceramic tile floor and wainscot offer good protection against occasional splashes from the tub.

Choosing a Whirlpool Tub

WHIRLPOOL TUBS ARE AVAILABLE in a wide range of sizes, styles, and prices, so choosing the one that's right for you can be a daunting task. Here are a few points to consider:

- Don't get a larger tub than you need. Tubs can range in capacity from 50 gallons to over 200 gallons. Large tubs look great in the showroom, but they take a long time to fill and can tax even the largest hot-water systems.

- Get right in the tub at the showroom to try it out. Sitting in the tub will tell you if it is comfortable or not, and if it will have enough room for you and your partner.

- Choose a quality acrylic tub rather than a less-expensive fiberglass unit. Acrylic tubs look better longer because their color won't fade, and you'll be able to buff out minor scratches.

- Choose the size and number of jets that will give you the type of massaging action you want. Large-diameter jets placed high on the tub walls produce a gentle swirling action, while smaller-diameter jets introduce a more vigorous massage to specific points on the body. Options like neck and back massage jets can be a godsend to those with chronic back problems.

- Consider an in-line heater. If you plan on taking a long bath, in-line heaters can maintain a constant water temperature for as long as you stay in the tub.

- Think about control options. Digital controls mounted right on the tub for easy access are more convenient than wall-mounted controls. Multispeed and variable-speed pumps offer more flexibility than single-speed pumps.

▲DESIGNED TO FIT INTO A CORNER, this whirlpool tub has plenty of room for two but doesn't occupy too much floor space.

▶ A STEP DOWN FROM THE MASTER BEDROOM leads to this master bath, with an expansive whirlpool tub surrounded by glazed Mexican tiles as its centerpiece. The window is placed high on the wall to provide both privacy and natural light.

▼ RICHLY TEXTURED WOOD TRIM contrasts with the white-finished curved concrete walls of this side-by-side tub and shower. Water falls like a gentle rain from the oversized showerhead suspended from the ceiling, helping to reduce splash and overspray from this open shower.

Worth the Risk?

ARE WHIRLPOOL TUBS HAZARDOUS TO YOUR HEALTH? According to some studies, conventional whirlpool pipes can be a breeding ground for harmful bacteria, including e.coli, staphylococcus, and legionella. Known as biofilm, the mix can contaminate the water, and even the air, in and around a whirlpool.

Most whirlpool tub manufacturers dismiss these claims, stating that complaints about tub contamination have been minor and current cleaning and purging protocols solve most of the problems. Most manufacturers recommend a regular cleaning program; for example, Kohler® advises their tub owners to purge their whirlpools twice a month with two teaspoons of dishwasher detergent and four ounces of household bleach. The key, apparently, is to keep the biofilm from forming at all.

◀ A SPACE WITHIN A SPACE, this arched alcove has a deck that's cut out of a slab of honed Durango limestone, along with an under-mounted cast-iron tub. The mono-chromatic color scheme focuses attention on the art and decorative objects found in this combination bathing and dressing area.

An Accessible Bathtub

GETTING INTO AND OUT OF A TUB can be a major challenge for many people, and bathing safely should be a priority for everyone. There are several simple ways to optimize a standard bathtub so that it is more accessible for those with disabilities and safer for all. Tubs are hard and slippery, so securely attached grab bars are a good idea for all bathrooms, while a height-adjustable hand shower makes bathing and showering more comfortable from

either a standing or seated position (and is great for kids, too). Controls should be equipped with lever-type handles for ease of use, and should be mounted so that they can be operated from both inside and outside the tub.

For even more accessibility, some manufacturers offer tubs with door-type entry (photo below), making it much easier to enter and exit the bath. Watertight gaskets seal the door and keep bathwater in the tub when it's filled.

▲ ARJO'S FREEDOM BATHTUB features a Roll-Door that slides beneath the floor of the bath. When the door is in the fully raised position, an inflatable, watertight seal secures the door and won't deflate until all the water has drained from the tub.

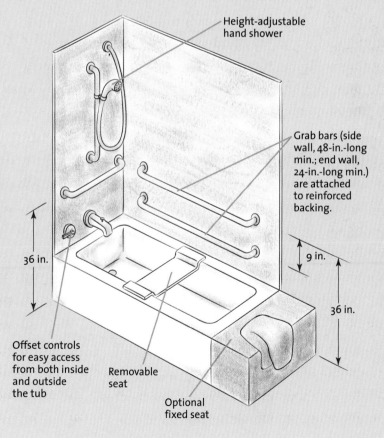

Height-adjustable hand shower

Grab bars (side wall, 48-in.-long min.; end wall, 24-in.-long min.) are attached to reinforced backing.

36 in.

9 in.

36 in.

Offset controls for easy access from both inside and outside the tub

Removable seat

Optional fixed seat

▶ A CERAMIC MOSAIC "RUG" inset into the tiled floor of this large master bathroom adds a touch of color and texture to the monochromatic color scheme. Removable panels underneath the tub deck provide easy access for servicing the pump and plumbing of the tub.

▼ IN THE DESERT, massive materials such as stone, concrete, and plaster and heat-reflecting shades of white are extensively used to help moderate temperature, an influence that is clearly seen in this expansive Southwest-style bathroom.

Porcelain Enamel

ONE EXPLANATION FOR THE ENDURING POPULARITY of vintage claw-foot tubs is their porcelain-enamel finish, a surface that has proven to be durable, sanitary, easy to clean, and highly resistant to chemicals and corrosion. Porcelain enamel starts out as a mixture of minerals that are heated and drawn out into a glasslike ribbon, then cooled and pulverized. The resulting particulate—or frit—is then sprayed onto a base metal (usually cast iron) and fired at high temperature, fusing the two materials together.

COMBINATION BATHS

◄CLEAR GLASS SHOWER DOORS, a large window and a built-in seating area attached to the far side of this standard 5-ft.-wide cast-iron tub makes the space larger, more practical, and more comfortable.

▲RENOVATED TO REFLECT the period character of this 19th-century house, this bathroom's countertop is honed Carrera marble, while the fabric of the shower curtain has a pin-dot pattern to match the tiles used in the tub-surround.

◄THOUGH IT'S ONLY 42 IN. LONG, this barrel-vaulted combination tub/shower is fully functional thanks to its extra width and custom bifold frameless shower door. Note the shower curtain over the window, which protects it from the indoor weather.

► THOUGH IT'S THE SAME LENGTH as a standard-size tub, this cast-iron tub is wider than normal and has an accompanying shelf built into the surround, giving this compact alcove a feeling of spaciousness. Faceted corners on the tub and tumbled-marble tile are simple but elegant touches.

Bathtub Makeover

I F YOU WANT A NEW COMBINATION TUB/SHOWER but don't want the hassle of tearing out your old tub, you might consider re-lining it with a new acrylic shell. Your local contractor can order and install a durable and easy-to-clean, custom-molded ¼-in.-thick acrylic liner right over an existing tub, as well as acrylic wall panels to match.

The shell comes from Luxury Bath Systems™, which has an inventory of over 400 vacuum molds (made from old bathtubs) that it uses to produce the shells. The process takes about a day and typically costs between $1,500 and $2,000, far less than the cost of demolition, buying a new tub, and the associated plumbing and carpentry costs that go along with the process.

▲ IT USUALLY ONLY TAKES ABOUT A DAY to give an old bathtub a facelift with a new acrylic liner.

A Retractable Curtain Rod

ONE PROBLEM WITH COMBINATION TUB/SHOWERS is managing the spray from the shower-head. Shower curtains or shower doors are the typical solutions, but both occupy a lot of visual space, especially if the room is small. Builder Jim Garramone took an innovative approach to solving this dilemma by designing a retractable curtain rod that allows the curtain to fold back neatly against the wall.

The rod is a 10-ft.-long stainless-steel tube that slides on a pair of flange-mounted linear bearings fastened to blocks behind the wall where there's unoccupied attic space (this setup requires unoccupied space behind the wall to work). When it's needed, a gentle tug on the curtain easily pulls the rod out from the wall, where it then cantilevers out over the tub. The tubing has thick 0.065-in. walls, so the rod won't deflect when it is fully extended.

◀▲WHEN THE CURTAIN ROD IS RETRACTED, the shower curtain tucks unobtrusively up against the wall (left). A gentle tug on the curtain pulls the 10-ft. stainless-steel curtain rod out from the wall, gliding easily on its bearings (above).

BEYOND THE BASIC BATH

▲ PART OF AN ADDITION that also houses an art collection, this lap pool is covered with small blue glass tiles from Mexico. The pool cantilevers out 10 ft. from the zinc-clad skin of this Boston-area home.

▲ LIKE AN OUTDOOR LIVING ROOM with a pool running through it, the courtyard of this Palm Springs residence connects the main house and guest house and is shaded by a curved canopy overhead. A waterfall springing from the lower trellis casts a cooling mist over this desert pool, which remains shaded in the heat of the day.

▶ WITH A FLIP OF A SWITCH, an electrically operated cover rolls back to reveal this spacious hot tub. Part of an addition that also includes an exercise area, the room has a tumbled-marble tile floor, a cherry-paneled ceiling, and silk fabric wall coverings.

◀PART OF THE BATHROOM but off in its own special world, this sunken spa is surrounded on four sides by views through the trees.

Endless Summer

THERE'S NO QUESTION THAT SWIMMING is great exercise and that hydrotherapy is good for both the body and the soul. But instead of heading for your local health club or a nearby beach, how about a pool that fits in your garage or basement? For about the price of a minivan, the Endless Pool is compact enough at 8 ft. by 15 ft. to fit just about anywhere indoors or outdoors.

The pool consists of six 14-gauge galvanized steel panels that bolt together on site to form a 7-ft. by 14-ft. by 39-in.-high freestanding swim area. The enclosure is lined with a 28-mil PVC liner that's 50-percent thicker than standard swimming pool liners, while a 5-HP water-propulsion system creates an adjustable current that you swim against. The standard kit also includes a water heater and filtration system. The only question is, how do you tell how many laps you've done?

▲THIS COMPACT POOL creates an adjustable current so that you can swim endless laps in your own home.

Showers

WHEN THERE'S ENOUGH ROOM, it's a good idea to design your bathroom with separate showering and bathing areas. Compared to combination tub/showers, a separate walk-in shower is generally larger and easier to enter and exit, making it safer and more comfortable to use. Spaces that are used only for showering are also easier to keep clean (no bathtub ring), while larger showers can be equipped with benches for seating and multiple showerheads and body jets for more versatility. With the range of enclosure options available, from glass panels to glass-block walls to traditional tiled walls, a beautiful and functional shower enclosure can fit into just about any bathroom.

▼A GOOD EXAMPLE of how different materials can be used innovatively in bathroom design, this shower's slightly curved walls are clad with galvanized sheet-metal roofing panels. Because the shower is large and has high curbs, it doesn't need a door.

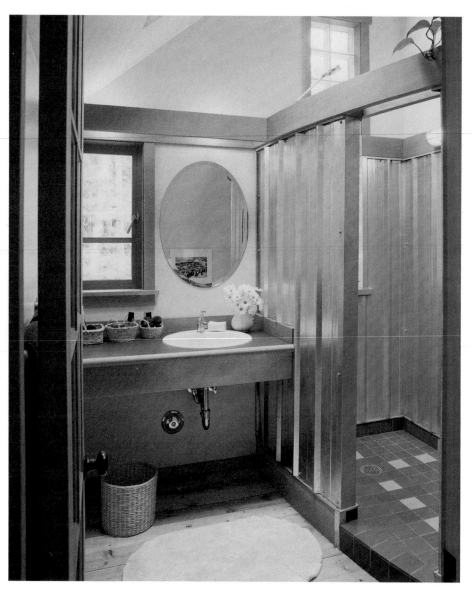

▲TUCKED UNDER THE STAIRS of a renovated Brooklyn carriage house, this first-floor shower makes good use of space that might otherwise be wasted.

◀▲▲ A COLORFUL RAINBOW of glass tile lines the interior and exterior of this circular shower, which acts as an airlock entryway into an adjoining pool room. Much of the trimwork for the shower—the doorjambs, for example—is made of Corian, a solid-surface material that can be shaped with standard woodworking tools but has the properties of stone. The pebble-stone floor inside the shower and the ceramic-tile floor on the outside are both radiantly heated.

▲ IT WOULD BE A SHAME to hide the gorgeous stone and tile work in this walk-in shower, making frameless glass a good choice for the enclosure. This shower is also equipped with a steam generator, a good antidote for the aches and pains of daily life.

MANUFACTURED SHOWERS

▲MANUFACTURED SHOWERS are available in a number of configurations. This corner shower consists only of the base and the glass enclosure; it's a good choice in a confined bathroom because it utilizes limited floor area effectively without occupying a lot of visual space. Because the walls of this shower must be tiled on site, it can be customized to match a bathroom's décor.

▲THIS FULL-FEATURED WHIRLPOOL TUB and integral shower offers room for two, multiple showerheads and body jets, a steam-bath option, a built-in stereo system, and an optional TV monitor, yet occupies only a little more floor space than a conventional tub.

◄AN EXAMPLE of the one-piece roofed construction that is characteristic of an acrylic shower, this unit features built-in bench seating and a barrier-free design.

Gelcoat versus Acrylic

THEY LOOK THE SAME IN THE SHOWROOM, but there's a reason why acrylic showers and tubs cost more than gelcoat units. While they're manufactured out of essentially the same materials, the difference lies in how they're put together.

Gelcoat units (see the top left photo) start out on a mold that is first sprayed with a thin, $\frac{1}{64}$-in. layer of pigmented resin; this is the gelcoat and the surface that you actually see when you step into the shower. Then layers of fiberglass mixed with resin are added on top of the gelcoat until it is about $\frac{1}{8}$-in. thick so that it's structurally sound. Before the unit is removed from the mold, various reinforcing "inclusions"—foam, wood, even cardboard—are added for structural rigidity (see top right photo).

Acrylic units (see the center photos) start out as a $\frac{1}{8}$-in.-thick sheet of acrylic, which is heated, stretched over a mold, then sucked into shape with vacuum pressure. After the acrylic shell cools, the same kinds of fiberglass reinforcing and inclusions are added to give it strength and rigidity (see the bottom photo). Because of the way they're built, acrylic units usually have ceilings, while fiberglass ones don't.

Acrylic units cost more than twice as much as their gelcoat counterparts, but offer more durability and scratch and fade resistance. In fact, slight scratches in acrylic tubs can be sanded and buffed out.

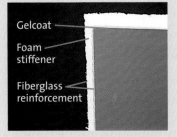

▲ FIBERGLASS TUBS have a thin layer of gelcoat, a polyester resin, which gives the tub its color and smooth finish.

◄ ECONOMICAL AND LIGHTWEIGHT, gelcoat fiberglass tub/showers are available in a wide range of sizes, colors, and configurations.

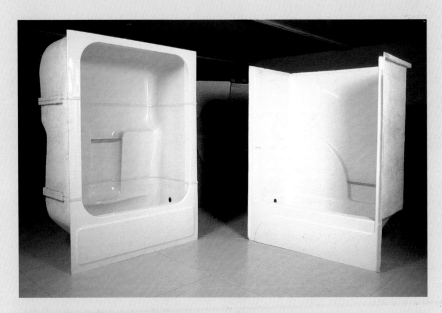

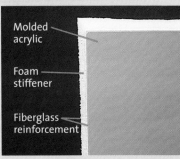

▲ MOLDED ACRYLIC TUB/SHOWERS cost more than twice as much as gelcoat tubs but offer better durability and fade resistance.

◄ THE THICKER LAYER OF MOLDED ACRYLIC is what gives an acrylic tub/shower its durability.

▲ A MINIMAL FRAMELESS GLASS divider panel and door shields the vanity from the tub and shower enclosure in this bathroom, a design that keeps wet areas wet and dry areas dry without blocking natural light or making the bathroom feel smaller.

▶ A SINGLE 9-ft. by 4-ft. panel of acid-etched, tempered glass is the only thing separating this shower from the rest of the bathroom. The key to this curbless design is a waterproof, well-drained floor that pitches toward a central drain, and walls that are covered with 1¼-in.-thick granite.

▲THIS OPEN SHOWER is nearly outside, with large custom-built doors that lead to a private yard and a slate-covered shower tower. Kneewalls of concrete and glass block on each side of the shower help keep splashes under control.

AN ACCESSIBLE SHOWER

Hand-held shower should be mounted on an adjustable track and be no higher than 48 in. above the floor in its lowest position.

A shower designed for universal accessibility is easier and safer for everyone to use. For example, an adjustable-height hand-held shower makes showering more comfortable for people of all sizes and abilities, while offset shower controls away from the water flow can be easily reached from both inside and outside the shower.

Shower seat (15 in. wide max.) is 17 in. to 19 in. above the floor and folds out of the way when not in use.

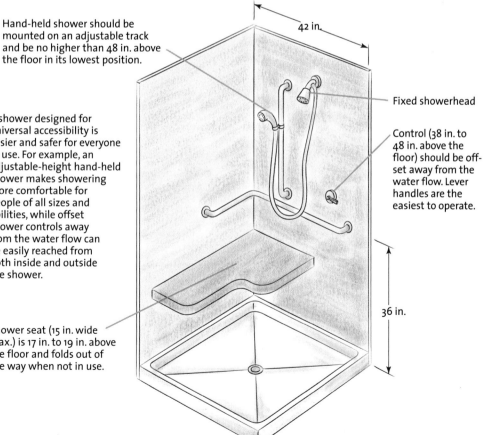

42 in.

Fixed showerhead

Control (38 in. to 48 in. above the floor) should be off-set away from the water flow. Lever handles are the easiest to operate.

36 in.

▶ COLUMNS FRAME THE ENTRANCE to this elegant shower finished with gold-plated fixtures and full-sized slabs of Carrara marble. Impurities in the marble are what give it its characteristic veining and hints of color, and because Carrara marble contains small amounts of iron that oxidize when in contact with oxygen, it will turn slightly brownish-yellow over time.

Slippery When Wet

A WET FLOOR is a potentially very slippery floor, particularly if smooth high-gloss tiles have been installed instead of more appropriate slip-resistant tiles. One solution is to tear up the tiles and start over. Another solution is to try applying Y-Slip™, a two-part product applied directly to tile that in some cases can increase traction underfoot. It's also possible to apply a new layer of floor tile over the existing tile, but this tricky procedure should only be done by an experienced tile contractor.

Invisible Curtain Rod

FRAMELESS SHOWER DOORS are beautiful but expensive, with some costing $3,000 to $4,000. Shower curtains are a cheaper alternative, but many don't like the look of the hardware that the curtain hangs from. Architect Stephen Vanze came up with this relatively easily built alternative, a kind of valance that spans the opening and has a channel running down the middle of it. A conventional shower rod hides in the 6-in. by 6-in. recess centered in the bottom edge of the valance, and the curtain is hung from it with regular curtain hooks. This is one way to add a touch of class to a bath without spending a lot of cash.

▶THIS SHOWER CURTAIN HANGS from a conventional shower rod hidden in a recess framed into the valance over the shower entrance.

◀LARGE ENOUGH FOR THE WHOLE FAMILY, this tempered-glass shower enclosure has multiple body jets, an adjustable hand shower, and a fixed showerhead.

Shower Enclosures and Doors

TEMPERED-GLASS SHOWER ENCLOSURES are an elegant and effective way of keeping water where it belongs. They're adaptable to many different types of showers, easy to clean, and can actually help make a bathroom feel larger.

Shower enclosures come in two basic varieties: framed and frameless. Frameless systems are popular because of their clean look, but they are more expensive, requiring thicker glass, costly hardware, and professional fabrication. Framed systems are stronger and cost less, use lighter-weight glass, and are more forgiving during installation. A standard, high-quality framed sliding door will cost around $175 (not including installation). An equivalent frameless slider runs about $400 uninstalled.

Both framed and frameless enclosures require hardware; the difference is that frameless hardware is a lot less obtrusive (see photos below left). Besides choosing a finish for the hardware, you'll also need to determine whether the enclosure door will slide or hinge. Fortunately, track designs for sliding doors have improved considerably over the years; look for doors that use stainless-steel flanges and ride on sealed, ball-bearing rollers inside either an aluminum or brass track (see photo below right).

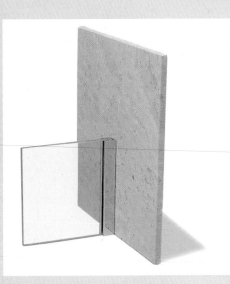

▶ SLIDING DOORS RIDE ON ROLLERS inside a brass or aluminum track. Tracks can have different finishes for different looks, including (from top to bottom) powder-coated aluminum, gold-anodized aluminum, chrome-anodized aluminum, chrome-plated brass, nickel-plated brass, and brushed-nickel-plated brass.

▲ ▶ FRAMELESS SHOWER enclosures still require some sort of hardware to hold the tempered-glass panels in place. The deeper aluminum channels (above) are the easiest to work with and can hide an out-of-plumb wall, while wall-mount clamps (right) have minimal visual impact but require notching or drilling.

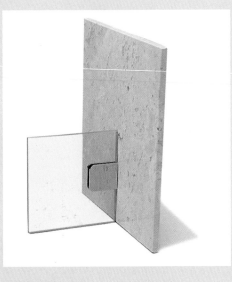

Shower stalls require hinged doors that swing outward, a configuration that drips water onto the floor when the door is opened unless there is a bottom gutter. There are a number of different possible hinge configurations for both framed and frameless doors, including wall- and glass-mounted hinges, as well as pivoting hinges that mount on the top and bottom of the glass instead of the side (see photos this page).

Finally, remember that the clear glass enclosures that look so elegant in the showroom are the hardest to keep clean. Water spots don't show up as easily on the various types of patterned or frosted translucent glass panels.

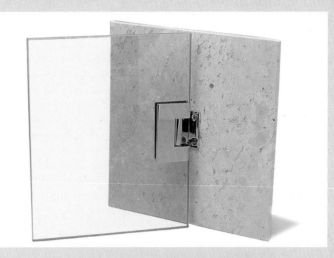

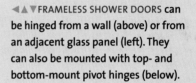

◀▲▼FRAMELESS SHOWER DOORS can be hinged from a wall (above) or from an adjacent glass panel (left). They can also be mounted with top- and bottom-mount pivot hinges (below).

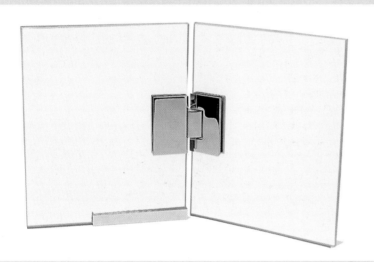

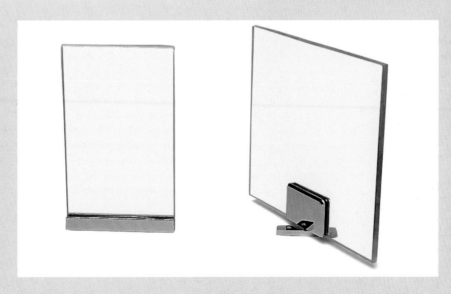

OUTDOOR SHOWERS

▶ARTICULATING SHOWERHEADS retract out of the way when this limestone entryway isn't being used as an outdoor shower.

▼LOCATED BETWEEN the main living area and a trellised patio, this bathroom serves as a transition between indoor and outdoor space.

◀ THE LAID-BACK LIFESTYLE of Southern California beckons from this cabana shower located in the Pasadena hills.

▲ CONNECTED TO THE BATHROOM inside by the doorway to the right, this outdoor shower also has a stainless-steel soaking tub and a simple galvanized-steel screen for privacy.

Water Therapy

THERE'S AN ELEMENTAL ATTRACTION to surf crashing on an ocean beach. The sound is rhythmic and overpowering, the motion of the waves almost hypnotic; you come away feeling awed and revitalized, energized by the combination of sun, water, and wind. To some extent an outdoor shower can re-create that environment. Scientists tell us that the secret is negative ionization, a beneficial process where free electrons attach themselves to other molecules. Electrical or metaphysical, sunshine and water are a great combination for recharging the spirit.

SAUNAS & STEAM SHOWERS

▲ ▶ THE NIGHTS ARE LONG AND
COLD in Alaska, making this
Japanese-inspired cedar bathhouse a treasured retreat for both
body and soul. Located close to
the Alaskan coast, the bathhouse
contains a sauna, a bathroom, and
a laundry room.

◀ALL SURFACES IN A STEAM SHOWER need to be impervious to moisture, and the shower needs to be completely enclosed so that steam doesn't escape into the rest of the bathroom. It's also a good idea to slope the ceiling to guide condensation toward the walls and away from your head and shoulders.

◀THE HEART OF A STEAM SHOWER is a steam generator, a suitcase-size (or smaller) electric boiler that can be hidden in a nearby vanity, closet, basement, or heated attic within about 25 ft. of the shower. Steam is piped into the shower through a simple steam head located near the bottom of the shower about 6 in. to 8 in. above the floor.

Sweat Therapy

WHAT'S SO HOT ABOUT SWEAT? Consider this: It's as essential as eating or breathing; if you eliminate the body's ability to sweat by smothering the skin, it dies within hours. Sweat rids the body of waste and regulates its temperature, and it keeps the skin clean and elastic. The problem is, most of us don't sweat enough. Air-conditioning, antiperspirants, and inactivity all conspire to keep us sweat-free.

Much like jogging or other forms of exercise, the heat of a steam bath or sauna urges every organ of the body into action. Blood vessels dilate, the heart rate and metabolism increases, and the body's core temperature rises, making it difficult for some bacterial and viral agents to survive. For once, something that feels so good is actually so good for you.

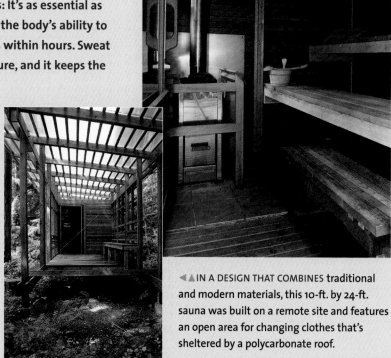

◀▲IN A DESIGN THAT COMBINES traditional and modern materials, this 10-ft. by 24-ft. sauna was built on a remote site and features an open area for changing clothes that's sheltered by a polycarbonate roof.

Faucets and Sprays

TUB AND SHOWER FIXTURES are safer, more durable, and more stylish than ever before. In fact, there are so many options now that choosing just the right faucet can be a real challenge. You'll probably want to coordinate with the sink faucet, but you'll also have to sort out options like hand-held showers and body sprays as well.

There are also finishes to consider. Polished chrome remains a popular favorite because of its durability and low maintenance, but the new brass finishes are just as durable. For a new look, consider one of the colored epoxy-coated finishes, which can give your faucets an exciting contemporary look.

▲ IN THIS CONTEMPORARY BATH, a disk rain shower is recessed into the ceiling of the spacious shower (built with stainless-steel panels and Spanish limestone).

◄ IN MOST BATHROOMS the plumbing and tub/shower valve are buried in the wall and hidden from view, but in this innovative tiled Roman tub the plumbing is part of the design. Simple gate valves, copper pipe, and standard fittings were used to create the assembly here, which doubles as a great place to hang washcloths.

▲ WITH A HALF-DOZEN SIZES AND SHADES of tile, this children's bath is an intricate composition in color and design, a look that is uncomplicated by the clean styling of these contemporary white tub and shower faucets. Hanging in the window over the tub is an aluminum grid containing hundreds of different colored marbles, a playful way of injecting the room with a kaleidoscope of light.

◄ PRACTICAL AS WELL AS STYLISH, this hand-held shower can also be used to water the plants in the window box and to wash down the shower's slate walls after cleaning.

▲ALTHOUGH YOUR TUB MIGHT BE meant for soaking, a hand shower is still a handy feature for washing hair, rinsing off afterward, and cleanup. This one has a classic polished brass finish.

◀▲MOUNTED ON A TUB DECK carved out of an exquisite slab of Carrera marble, this ornate, gold-plated Roman faucet with matching handles has a higher capacity than an ordinary tub faucet, enabling it to quickly fill the tub. A mirrored alcove amplifies the light and views of the nearby harbor while carving out this intimate bathing niche from a large master bathroom.

▼ THE POLISHED CHROME FINISH on this combination hand shower and tub faucet is nearly indestructible and can stand up to abrasive cleaners and water with high mineral content.

▲ ONE DISADVANTAGE OF A CLAW-FOOT TUB is that there is no deck space for keeping bathing essentials nearby. This wire basket accessorizes the tub's polished chrome faucet nicely and is a handy place for storing wet soaps and sponges. A space-saving alternative to a separate piece of furniture, the maple-trimmed shelves slide out only when they're needed.

SHOWER FAUCETS

▲SOME SHOWERHEADS are designed to provide a pressure-assisted hydromassage, but this large showerhead relies on gravity to deliver a gentle soaking that feels like a rain shower instead of a car wash.

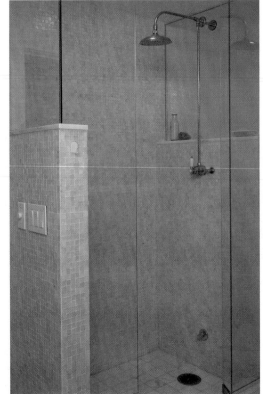

▲BECAUSE THESE SHOWERHEADS are mounted on tracks, they can be adjusted so that they're comfortable to use regardless of the user's height. Twin shower valves give each user control over the water's temperature.

◀AN EXPOSED RISER from the shower valve to the oversize showerhead is mounted on the glass panel wall of this shower enclosure. The brass fixture mounted toward the base of the wall is a steam showerhead.

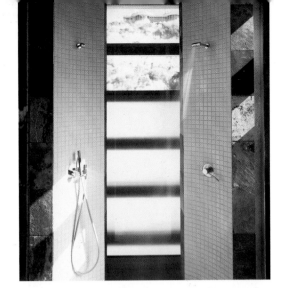

►THIS SEMICIRCULAR SHOWER'S OPEN DESIGN features two separate shower controls, giving each user the ability to control water temperature, volume, and spray type.

Anti-Scald Valves

ANTI-SCALD VALVES are required by code in most new or renovated bathrooms. There are two basic types: pressure-balancing valves and thermostatic valves. Pressure-balancing valves are the least expensive and most widely available; they work by detecting and compensating for sudden pressure changes between the hot and cold water supplies.

Thermostatic valves maintain a constant water-output temperature regardless of the temperature or the water pressure of the hot and cold water supplies. Most thermostatic valves have an integral volume control, and some of them can be set to a preselected temperature.

There are plenty of cheap anti-scald valves that offer some degree of protection, but they don't work as smoothly, quickly, or reliably as the better valves. Though expensive, a good valve is still cheap insurance against scalds or injuries.

◄A SINGLE plumbing connection feeds this water tower, which has telescoping shower arms, height-adjustable body sprays, and a hand-held shower.

Toilets and Sinks

Consider this: It wasn't until shortly after the end of World War I that building codes in the United States began requiring bathrooms and indoor plumbing. Before that, outhouses, chamber pots, and Saturday night scrubs in the kitchen washtub were the rule rather than the exception. Now, of course, bathrooms have come out of the closet, and most households have more than one of them; they're an integral part of the American home.

If exquisite tubs and showcase showers are the stars in a bathroom production, toilets and sinks have long been considered the supporting cast. Day in and day out, they've been expected to do the dirty work, look good while doing it, and be easily cleaned up afterward. In addition, water conservation has become—and rightly so—an increasingly important issue; new toilets are required by law to use less than half the amount of water as their predecessors.

As you'll see on the following pages, manufacturers have responded, offering new materials, technologies, and innovations in design and engineering for these once-prosaic fixtures. Toilets and sinks are ready for prime time, playing their roles with more style and efficiency than ever before.

◄ THIS TWO-PIECE TOILET with sculpted lines and matching bidet commands a great view of both the interior and exterior of this large master bath suite. The small cast-iron sink is supported by wrought-iron supports and has a large kitchen-style faucet with a pull-out spray mounted on the deck behind it.

Toilets and Bidets

IRST DEVELOPED BACK IN THE MID-19TH CENTURY, early toilets weren't perfect. For one thing, they tended to leak dangerous methane sewer gas back into the home, sometimes with explosive results. Toward the end of the century, manufacturers began producing vitreous-china toilets with flush valves, solving that problem and introducing designs that are still used today.

A century later, the toilet was on the hot seat again, with many complaining that the newly mandated 1.6 gpf (gallons per flush) toilets weren't up to the task and required double flushing. Fortunately, today's toilets work reliably while conserving water; some of them wash and dry you, play music, and automatically raise and lower their lids. Best of all, none of them explode.

▲ A LOW-PROFILE, ONE-PIECE TOILET like this offers distinct design opportunities, such as the ability to run a continuous countertop above it without affecting the ability to reach under the hood of the toilet when repairs are necessary.

◀ PART OF TOTO'S® CARROLLTON SUITE, this toilet and matching bidet are an example of how manufacturers create fixtures that share styling details, giving you the ability to create a coordinated look in your bathroom. This particular design features an unusual "skirt" around the base of the toilet, a feature that hides the trapway and makes the toilet easier to clean.

▼WHEN THIS QUEEN ANNE–STYLE VERMONT FARMHOUSE was built in 1890, a bathroom with a washout-style water closet and hot and cold running water would have been considered quite progressive for a rural area. Encasing the tinned copper tub with beadboard paneling to match the wainscot was a common practice at the time, when bathroom fixtures often were manufactured to look like furniture.

▲DESPITE THEIR CHARMS, outhouses have a well-deserved reputation for being dark, smelly, and filled with bugs and spiders; it's no wonder that most have disappeared or been converted into tool sheds or lawn ornaments. But this contemporary, open-air design features a composting toilet and mirrored mosaics, making it a compelling destination for when nature calls.

TOLIET OPTIONS

◀WHILE THIS HALF-WALL doesn't provide total privacy, it does visually separate this two-piece toilet from the rest of the bathroom. This toilet has an elongated rather than a round bowl, which adds about 2 in. to its overall length but makes it more comfortable to use.

▲A CLASSIC COMBINATION in a compact bathroom, this one-piece toilet and matching pedestal sink can share limited floor space without getting in each other's way.

▶ONLY A CURVED, GLASS-BLOCK HALF-WALL separates the shower from the toilet stall in this bathroom, a design that stylishly provides privacy without making either space feel cramped or confined.

◄THIS LOW-PROFILE, ONE-PIECE
TOILET has a top-mounted flush
lever integrated into the lid of the
toilet. Its contemporary styling is
a good match for the glass and
steel vanity.

Do Toilets Need a Separate Space?

THERE ARE TWO SCHOOLS OF THOUGHT when it comes to toilet placement. One point of view is that toilets should be sequestered, offering more privacy when a larger bathroom is used simultaneously by a couple and separating the two very different functions of elimination and personal hygiene.

The other point of view is that most bathrooms are used by only one person at a time anyway; a separate room for the toilet just wastes space and makes the user feel confined to a closet. To help you decide where you stand (or sit) on this issue, think about how you and your family actually use the bathrooms in your house.

▲IF A BATHROOM HAS TO SERVE more than one person at a time, consider a separate enclosure for the toilet.

▶ LOOKING MUCH LIKE IT DID when it was built back in 1884, this bathroom features a reproduction toilet with a tank located high on the wall, a design that provided a gravity-assisted boost to the flushing action of early toilets.

AN ACCESSIBLE TOILET

Most toilet seats are only 14½ in. off the floor, which is a little too low for those who have difficulty sitting down and standing up again. Higher 16-in. toilets are available, while grab bars make it easier and safer for everyone to use a toilet. Remember to leave enough room around the toilet; 15 in. from the centerline of the toilet to the wall is the minimum, but an accessible toilet will have 18 in. of clearance, as shown.

Back-wall grab bar is 36-in. long (min.); sidewall grab bar is 42-in. long (min.).

Grab bars are attached to reinforced backing.

Toilet-paper dispenser is 36 in. (max.) from the back wall and 26 in. from the floor.

36 in.

18 in.

An elongated bowl and a 16-in. seat height make access easier and more comfortable for wheelchair users.

◄WITH A BLACK TILE FLOOR punctuated by colorful glass accents and glass blocks strategically placed in the curved exterior wall, this toilet alcove is anything but ordinary. That's why it doesn't have an ordinary white toilet.

Evaluating the Latest Toilets

FLUSHING PERFORMANCE is a big issue in toilets lately. Time was, all toilets pretty much worked equally well, because flaws in toilet design and manufacturing were easily covered up by water—and plenty of it. There's not a lot that can stand in the way of $3\frac{1}{2}$ to 7 gallons of water rushing down a 3-in. or 4-in. drain. But with the National Energy Policy Act of 1992 cutting water consumption down to 1.6 gallons per flush, flaws in toilet engineering began to rise to the surface.

The solution to the demands of both clean water and clean toilet bowls is better toilet engineering. Where manufacturers once could crank out toilet after toilet with a design that had scarcely changed in almost 100 years, the low-flush mandate sent them back to their drawing boards. Instead of simply reconfiguring older toilets to use less water (like the first wave of low-flush toilets), they've turned to hydraulic engineers and computer modeling. The result? Better toilets that work more efficiently and offer more features and options than those produced even a decade ago.

Terry Love, a plumbing contractor in Redmond, Washington, has made it his business to evaluate the new toilets. Besides the ones he installs, he tests various models in the three bathrooms in his own home and solicits feedback from other plumbers around the country. Unlike a lot of plumbing contractors and retailers, he's not afraid to name names of both good and bad toilets, and he backs up his recommendations with personal and anecdotal experience on his Web site. For Terry's picks and pans, visit his Web site at www.terrylove.com.

▲TOTO'S PLYMOUTH TOILET combines traditional styling with a one-piece design. Slightly taller than a standard toilet, this ADA-compliant toilet is one of Terry Love's recommended models.

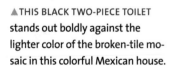
▲THIS BLACK TWO-PIECE TOILET
stands out boldly against the
lighter color of the broken-tile mosaic in this colorful Mexican house.

▲REFLECTED IN THE BEVELED MIRRORS lining the walls
of this powder room is a black and white toilet, a
unique look created by combining the tank of a black
toilet with the bowl of a white toilet.

◀A PROPERLY INSTALLED TOILET shouldn't leak, but
in warm humid weather, cold water that enters the
toilet after each flush causes condensation to occur
on the cooled surfaces of the toilet tank. To prevent
damage to wood floors, designer David Edrington
installs a marble saddle under the toilet; condensation drips harmlessly onto the saddle—where it
evaporates—rather than onto the wood.

▲COMPOSTING TOILETS work differently than flushing toilets, though they don't look all that different. While there's no water in the bowl, which makes it a little harder to clean, it's quieter because it doesn't flush (and no, it doesn't smell like an outhouse).

What's New in Toilet Design?

THE JAPANESE LEAD THE WAY in new toilet designs and innovations. As proof, consider the fact that more homes in Japan have toilet jet sprays than have personal computers. Here are some of the recent innovations unveiled by Japanese toilet makers in their battle to win over the hearts, minds, and bottoms of the Japanese people:

- A toilet seat equipped with electrodes that send a mild electric shock through the user's buttocks to measure body fat.
- A toilet that glows in the dark and automatically raises its lid when its infrared sensors detect a human nearby.
- A toilet that plays a user-selectable soundtrack when in use, including chirping birds, tinkling wind chimes, or the strumming of a traditional Japanese harp.
- A toilet that features twin air-conditioning and heating air nozzles. It can be programmed to heat or cool a bathroom to a set temperature at a pre-determined time.
- A toilet that automatically measures urine sugar levels by taking a collection with a retractable spoon.
- A toilet with a jet spray that is temperature- and pressure-programmable, which is used to wash and massage the buttocks.

▲THOUGH IT HAS A CONVENTIONAL APPEARANCE, Briggs's® Vacuity® toilet earns high marks for flushing performance thanks to a vacuum-assist system that is simpler and quieter than pressure-assisted 1.6 gpf toilets. This toilet is also available in one-piece and ADA-compliant versions.

▶ TOTO'S CHLOE WASHLET SEAT brings bidet-like features to a conventional toilet, including a seat warmer and an aerated water spray with temperature and volume controlled by the seat-mounted touchpad. The seat comes in round and elongated versions to fit most toilets.

BIDETS

▼THE TRADITIONAL LOOK of this bathroom is matched by the traditional lines of the two-piece toilet and bidet. The bidet has a deck-mounted horizontal-spray bidet valve, which operates much like a conventional sink faucet.

▲TOILETS AND BIDETS don't have to be placed side by side. In this bathroom, the sink is flanked on one side by the bidet and on the other by a toilet (not shown).

◄THIS BIDET FEATURES a simple, horizontal-spray valve with a white finish—a clean and simple look that's a perfect complement to this contemporary bath.

Bidet Valve Options

BIDETS REQUIRE SOMETHING THAT **toilets don't: a valve to turn the water on and off while you use the bidet. If you've decided on a bidet, you'll also** have to decide on the type and style of bidet valve that you want.

The simplest and least expensive type of bidet valve is the deck-mounted horizontal-spray bidet faucet. This valve is similar in design and function to a standard sink faucet and mounts on the back of the bidet. When turned on, water sprays out from the valve spout only, though a pop-up stopper in the fixture itself can be used to retain water in the bowl. Bidet faucets can have either a single or double control (see photo top right).

Vertical-spray bidet valves are a bit more complicated. Fresh water from the mixing valve is sprayed from a sprinkler—or "rose"—located in the bowl of the fixture, so these valves require a vacuum breaker (the drumlike or cylindrical contraption located near the back of some bidets) to keep contaminated water from back-siphoning into the fresh water supply. Depending on the style of the bidet, this type of valve can be mounted either on the back of the bidet like a horizontal-spray faucet, or in the wall behind the fixture (see photo bottom right).

▲SOMEWHAT UNUSUAL FOR A BIDET, this one features a lid. It has a horizontal-spray valve mounted on the deck, which operates essentially like a sink faucet.

▲THE BIDET IN THIS MATCHING SET has a vertical-spray bidet valve, with water spraying from a sprinkler located in the bowl of the fixture.

◄IN THIS SPACIOUS MASTER BATH-ROOM there's plenty of room for both a toilet and a bidet. This bidet has a vertical-spray valve, with water sprayed from a sprinkler in the front of the bowl.

Sinks

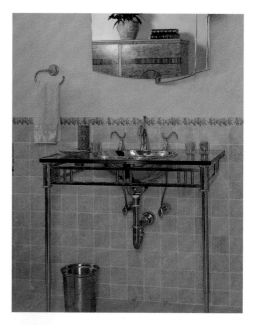

ABEAUTIFUL SINK CAN BE A FOCAL POINT in any bathroom, but because of the hard use that sinks receive, there has to be substance behind the style. Vanity-mounted sinks are popular because they offer the most storage and countertop space. On the other hand, new materials and designs have prompted a resurgence in popularity for wall-hung sinks, which are also the most accessible type of sink. And don't forget about freestanding pedestal-style sinks, which can be found in both classic and contemporary configurations to match the wide range of bathrooms being built today.

▲ WHILE BRUSHED STAINLESS STEEL is a more easily maintained finish, this polished stainless-steel sink looks great when combined with the sleek glass countertop. The open design of this sink sacrifices storage space but keeps the bathroom looking clean and uncluttered, emphasizing the beautiful stone-tile wainscot.

◄ INSPIRED BY THE WASHBASINS of the past, this graceful, table-mounted sink bowl is rooted in tradition yet decidedly contemporary.

▶LOCATED IN AN HISTORIC SEASIDE HOUSE built in the 19th century, this vanity design is a classic: his-and-her undermount sinks set into a Carrara marble countertop. Seashell marble mosaic accents in the floor are a playful reminder of the home's nautical connection.

▲THIS PAIR OF ENAMELED CAST-IRON SINKS are mounted on wrought-iron brackets. Each one has an oversize kitchen faucet with a pull-out spray mounted on a Carrera marble deck behind the sink.

◀THIS ASYMMETRICAL EUROPEAN SINK has a matte finish and a lot of surface area for storage; it's mounted on a custom mahogany and cherry vanity. The guest bathroom that it's in has a slate floor and glass-tile wainscot.

VANITY-MOUNTED SINKS

▲ FITTED INTO AN ALCOVE, this green-painted vanity is topped with a stone mosaic-tile countertop and a drop-in, hand-painted ceramic bowl sink.

▲ TO FIT IN A NARROW POWDER ROOM, Architect Stephen Bobbitt designed a shallow, 18-in.-deep vanity with a curved front to accommodate a custom-painted sink bowl.

◄ A MAJOR ADVANTAGE of a vanity-mounted sink is the large amount of storage available underneath. This matching set of cabinets feature lots of drawers for storage and easily maintained solid-surface countertops.

▲INSTEAD OF BEING PUSHED UP against a wall, these back-to-back vanities occupy center stage in this bath. They're topped by a solid-surface countertop with integral sinks and a shared mirror, and are lit from above by numerous recessed lights in the ceiling.

▼CUSTOM-DESIGNED AND FABRICATED with corrugated steel panels for the doors and sides and stainless-steel balls for feet, this vanity supports a blue pearl-granite countertop and aqua sandblasted-glass sink. The mirror above has a frame of brushed aluminum with glass-ball accents.

Sink Materials: What's the Difference?

- **Vitreous china:** Pedestal and wall-mounted sinks made out of vitreous china are virtually impervious to any type of cleanser that you can throw at them, though they can chip and crack over time.
- **Ceramic:** Many local potteries (and some larger manufacturers) are offering custom-glazed ceramic sinks. While fairly durable, they're more prone to chipping and cracking than vitreous china.
- **Enameled cast iron:** Tough as nails, these sinks won't crack, though the finish might chip if something hard is dropped in one.
- **Enameled steel:** Noisier and more apt to chip than cast iron, these sinks are relatively uncommon today.
- **Stainless steel:** While not common in bathrooms, these durable sinks are easy to clean and hide dirt well. Other metals—pewter, nickel, and even silver—are softer and require considerable maintenance.
- **Cultured stone:** Created by mixing crushed stone (like marble or granite) with polyester resins, some inexpensive cultured-stone sinks have a gelcoated finish to give the sink its color and texture. This gelcoat will fade, crack, and blister over time. More-expensive, non-gelcoated cast-polymer sinks that have a higher percentage of minerals (like quartz), making them more durable, are better.
- **Solid-surface materials:** Sinks made from Corian and other similar solid-surface materials are durable and repairable (scratches and stains can be sanded out), and they can be fabricated into seamless, easily maintained, one-piece countertops.

WALL-HUNG SINKS

▶ TUCKED INTO THE CORNER of a tiny powder room, this custom-fabricated stainless-steel sink saves even more space with an integrated towel rack.

▲ ORIGINALLY THE SINK CUTOUT from a kitchen counter, this cast-off granite slab makes an elegant and inexpensive countertop for an unusual and innovative wall-mounted sink.

◀ WHEN INDUSTRIAL-STRENGTH CLEANING is required, this sturdy, trough-style stainless-steel sink is up to the task. It's located in an informal multipurpose room that has laundry facilities as well as a shower and a toilet.

◀CORNER-MOUNTED WALL-HUNG
SINKS are a popular and practical
choice when quarters are cramped.

Planning an Accessible Sink

THERE ARE SEVERAL WAYS that conventional sinks can be adapted for universal use. For example, many sinks are mounted about 30 in. above the floor, which is a better height for children and for those in a seated position. On the other hand, most adults are more comfortable with sinks that are around 36 in. off the floor (the height of a standard kitchen countertop). If there is room for two sinks, consider mounting them at different heights so that there is both a high and low sink.

Wheelchair users also need room to approach the sink and room underneath for their knees. Wall-mounted sinks that offer at least 27 in. of clearance between the front lower edge of the sink and the floor are ideal for this purpose. Many of them are available with shrouds to protect the knees of users from hot pipes or rough surfaces.

One drawback to wall-hung and pedestal-mounted sinks is that they have limited countertop room, while vanity-mounted sinks have ample countertop space but no knee room underneath. Suspending a countertop between two flanking vanities and leaving free space beneath the sink is a good compromise that offers both countertop space and storage. Of course, countertops can also be supported by wall-mounted brackets.

When planning storage for a universally accessible bathroom, remember that the optimal height for storage is between 15 in. and 48 in. above the floor. Also, the mirror above the sink should either tilt or extend all the way to the top of the counter so that a person in a seated position can use it.

Wheelchair users need clear space beneath a sink for access to it; wall-hung sinks most easily meet recommended accessibility clearance requirements, though all sinks can be modified to make them more user-friendly. Lever-type faucet handles are easily operated by both small children and those with limited hand mobility.

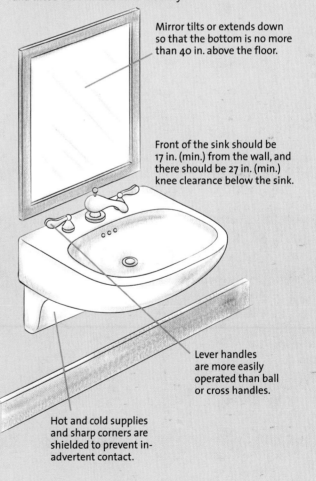

Mirror tilts or extends down so that the bottom is no more than 40 in. above the floor.

Front of the sink should be 17 in. (min.) from the wall, and there should be 27 in. (min.) knee clearance below the sink.

Lever handles are more easily operated than ball or cross handles.

Hot and cold supplies and sharp corners are shielded to prevent inadvertent contact.

FREESTANDING & PEDESTAL SINKS

▲RECYCLED FROM a 24-in.-dia. piece of PVC drainpipe, this sink base is painted with automotive lacquer and has a stainless-steel mixing bowl for a sink.

▶SUPPORTED BY A FRAMEWORK of galvanized steel pipe, this granite countertop has double under-mount sinks and wall-mounted faucets. While this bathroom has a modest floor plan, it feels large thanks to the mirror that extends all the way down to the counter-top, as well as high ceilings and clerestory windows.

◄ THIS OLD-FASHIONED SINK'S CLASSIC ELEGANCE makes it an appropriate choice in a wide range of bathroom styles.

▲ SIMPLE AND FUNCTIONAL, this small pedestal sink doesn't occupy much floor space in this small bathroom.

◄ WHILE IT LOOKS LIKE IT'S MADE OUT OF METAL, this pedestal is custom-molded acrylic and has a porcelain sink with a metallic, powder-coated finish. The floor and walls of this powder room are finished with thin, 2-ft. by 4-ft. sheets of marble stabilized by a fiberglass mat backing.

Selecting a Sink Height

JUST AS PEOPLE VARY IN SIZE, the height of your sink should vary too. In fact, you'll find that the height of so-called standard vanity cabinets is between 30 in. and 32 in., while many pedestal sinks will range between 32 in. and 36 in. Sinks used by shorter people and by children should be at the low end of the scale, while sinks used by taller people should be at the upper end of the scale.

Determining an ideal sink height for you and your family is just one part of the equation, however; finding the right sink configuration is the second part. Vanity-cabinet height can be increased by elevating the toekick area or by increasing the countertop thickness (or by a combination of both). Of course, wall-hung sinks can generally be installed at any elevation.

Many pedestal sinks are available with different-sized bases, though you might have to do a bit of searching to find a sink that is just the right height. Installing the pedestal on a raised platform is another way to raise the sink's height. If there are two sinks in a bathroom, the NKBA recommends installing them at different heights, depending on the needs of the user.

▲ SOME PEDESTAL SINKS are available with different-sized bases, so that you can vary their height above the floor.

▶ THESE PEDESTAL SINKS ARE RAISED UP on an inconspicuous marble platform that matches the floor, increasing their height and making them more comfortable to use by their tall owners.

◄ THE CONTEMPORARY STYLE of these European pedestal sinks is a good match for this clean, uncluttered bathroom. Each of the his-and-her sinks is set up in its own work area, with good task lighting and ample storage nearby.

▲ INSTEAD OF PORCELAIN CHINA, this pedestal sink is handcrafted out of wood. Slate-tile fingers in variegated shades (cut from the slate used on the floor and wall) decorate the edge of the countertop.

◄ PEDESTAL SINKS HAVE A CLASSIC LOOK but lack storage. Here, a freestanding antique cabinet, small medicine cabinet, and bracketed shelves make up the difference.

Faucets

CHOOSING A FAUCET AND CHOOSING A SINK go hand in hand. That's because most sinks need to be preconfigured for a specific type of faucet—single-hole, 4-in. spread, or 8-in. spread. As you look at the various types and styles of faucets, you'll notice a wide range of faucet finishes, handle designs, and spout types, too. It's important to look "under the hood" as well; ask questions about valve design and about the materials with which the faucet body is constructed. For instance, a solid-brass faucet will initially cost more than a plastic faucet with a chromed finish, but it can last a lifetime and will more than make up the difference with increased durability and better all-around performance.

▲ THIS UNIQUE SINK DESIGN exposes the plumbing and raises the spout high above the bowl, a nice feature if you wash your hair regularly in the sink.

◄ WATER FALLS FROM THIS WALL-MOUNTED FAUCET into a ceramic bowl sink. Two fir cabinets suspended from the wall support the polished granite countertop that supports the sink.

Faucet Styles

WITH THE WIDE RANGE OF STYLES **that are now being offered, it's difficult to categorize bathroom faucets, but you can't select a faucet without knowing the type of sink that it will be used with, and vice versa. For example, most faucets mount on the deck of the sink (see top photos and bottom left photo), but some sink bowls require a faucet that mounts on the wall behind the sink (see photo bottom right).**

Most faucets require three holes to be bored into the sink, countertop, or wall (see left photos), but some faucets require only a single hole (see photo top right); there are also a few faucet styles that require two holes (see photo bottom right). Again, you'll need to know the configuration of both your faucet and your sink, particularly if you're ordering a pre-bored porcelain or cast-iron sink.

Three-hole faucets that mount on widespread 8-in. (or more) centers are popular because it is easy to clean between the spout and the handles, and they look good on larger sinks. Regular 4-in. spread faucets often are used on smaller sinks and usually are packaged as a one-piece unit (see photo top left), though minispread faucets are also available.

▲ ONE-PIECE 4-IN. CENTERSET FAUCETS are a popular choice for smaller sinks.

▲ THIS UNUSUAL SINK has a deep bowl and a single-hole faucet with a high, swiveling gooseneck spout.

▲ THIS DECK-MOUNTED WIDESPREAD FAUCET has a high spout that makes it easier to wash the face and hands.

▲ THIS CERAMIC-BOWL SINK requires a wall-mounted faucet. It needs two mounting holes, one for the water control and one for the spout.

Faucet Valves

There are four basic types of faucet valves:
- Compression valves are the simplest type and found on traditional stem faucets. When the faucet handle is turned, a small rubber washer that seats against the bottom of the valve lifts, allowing water to flow.
- Sleeve cartridges were designed to replace compression valves and can be used in both single- and double-control designs. Although repairs are quick, replacement cartridges are sometimes difficult to find and can cost between $10 and $20, far more than the pennies needed for a new rubber washer on a stem faucet.

- Ball valves are often found on single-handle faucets. A hollow ball with three holes—two for the hot and cold water coming in and one for the mixed water going out to the spout—rotates within the faucet body. Varying the position of the ball with the handle varies the alignment of the holes, changing the mix of hot and cold and the volume of the water.
- Ceramic-disk cartridges are state-of-the-art and now widely used in all types of faucets. The cartridges consist of two highly polished ceramic disks with small openings through which water flows. Rotating the disks moves the holes into or out of alignment, increasing or decreasing the flow of water through the cartridge.

◀THE LOOK IS CLASSIC, THE DESIGN SIMPLE. Machined from solid brass and plated with a durable chrome finish that will last for decades, this widespread stem faucet has compression valves fitted with inexpensive and easily replaced rubber washers.

▲METALLIC FAUCET FINISHES, look elegant when new, but unless they've been applied to a faucet using new PVD technology, they need to be carefully maintained to prevent staining and tarnishing.

▶THIS UNUSUALLY SHAPED FAUCET has a brushed-bronze finish and is set into a honed Mexican travertine countertop and mahogany cabinet.

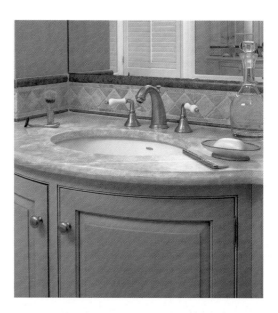

▼THIS WIDESPREAD FAUCET has a brushed-nickel finish and porcelain handles. Besides being more appropriately scaled for larger sinks, widespread faucets have a large gap between the handles and spout, making them easier to keep clean.

▲MOUNTED HIGH ON THE WALL, this sleek Vola® faucet has minimal visual impact, allowing the dramatic sink bowl to take center stage in this simple yet stylish powder room. The countertop is a slab of white statuary marble, while the floor is tiled with tumbled-marble mosaics.

▶WALL-MOUNTED FAUCETS offer unique design possibilities. This is a striking sink, but it's probably not practical for much more than gentle hand washing with no countertop to catch splashing water.

Faucet Finishes

BECAUSE IT WON'T SCRATCH OR CORRODE, polished chrome is an ideal faucet finish. No matter how grimy chrome fixtures become, they clean up easily with water, a sponge, and a little abrasive cleaner (see top photo).

Many people prefer the look of polished brass to chrome, but unprotected brass oxidizes when it comes in contact with air. Clear protective lacquer and epoxy coatings help control tarnishing, but they don't stand up well to abrasive cleansers. Now, however, through a new technology called physical vapor deposition (PVD), manufacturers can offer a shiny brass finish that has virtually the same durability as chrome. Different manufacturers call their PVD brass finishes by different names, but most offer lifetime warranties against tarnishing, corroding, or flaking. PVD technology is used for other polished or satin metallic faucet finishes as well (see center photo).

Colored-epoxy finishes are also popular, particularly in white. These baked-on finishes are durable and easy to clean, though not as scratch resistant as either chrome or brass. Abrasive cleaners should also be avoided with this type of finish (see bottom photo).

◄POLISHED CHROME IS A CLASSIC faucet finish that's extremely durable and easy to clean.

◄WHEN APPLIED USING A NEW TECHNOLOGY called physical vapor deposition, polished brass and other types of metallic finishes are just as durable as chrome. Many manufacturers guarantee them for the lifetime of the faucet.

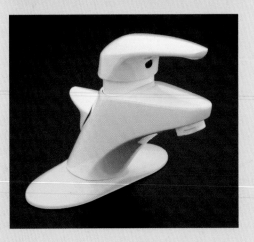

◄WHILE NOT QUITE AS DURABLE AS CHROME, powder-coated epoxy finishes offer a clean, contemporary look.

◀LOOKING LIKE IT'S FLOATING IN MID-AIR, this mirror-mounted faucet has a minimal presence that doesn't detract from the clean and uncluttered look of the glass sink and countertop.

▼INSTEAD OF AN ACTUAL FAUCET, this sink's water supply flows through ½-in. copper pipe and is controlled by a couple of gate valves that are normally used for rough plumbing.

▲REMINISCENT OF THE APOTHE-CARY'S MORTAR AND PESTLE, this ceramic faucet has a delicate and distinctive look.

Storage Solutions

R egardless of its size, any good bathroom design includes plenty of storage options. While we most often think of vanities and medicine cabinets when we think of bathroom storage, don't hesitate to think outside the box: Shelving, freestanding furniture, closets, towel bars and hooks, and even nooks and crannies in various combinations can all provide useful and appropriate storage.

When planning your bathroom's storage, keep in mind the many items that get used by all of the members of your household (or at least by those who will most often be using that bath). Medicine, toothpaste and toothbrushes, extra soap and shampoo, towels, toilet paper, first-aid supplies, cleaning products, cosmetics, and shaving gear all need a home. As you plan your bathroom's storage, also remember that some items are used often, while others are used infrequently; some items are quite small, while others are bulky. The best bathroom storage solutions provide a well-organized, easily accessible place for everything, regardless of whether the bathroom is spacious or compact.

◀ THE RENOVATED MASTER BATH OF THIS HISTORIC NANTUCKET HOUSE features two approaches to bathroom storage, with a useful cabinet of shallow drawers flanking a simple white vanity and providing easy-to-access storage. The accompanying pedestal sink on the left has a medicine cabinet with a small open shelf, a great place for keeping often-used items.

Cabinetry

CABINETS PLAY TWO ROLES in a bathroom: They provide out-of-sight storage for items of all shapes and sizes, and they help define the look of the bathroom. Doing both jobs with style is the trick.

Vanities are the basic storage building block; they can be fitted with drawers, shelves, tilt-out hampers, and other specialized accessories to maximize their storage capacity and efficiency. Medicine cabinets offer more easily accessible storage for smaller items, while open shelving is an underutilized option for colorful items like towels and shampoo bottles.

When choosing cabinetry, think about your particular storage needs, about how much room is available, and about the look you're trying to create.

▼ WITH PLENTY OF DRAWERS and a convenient central seating area, this stone-topped double vanity offers his-and-her storage that is close at hand. There's a heating duct in the toekick area of the cabinets—a good way to bring warmth to the cool tile and stone surfaces in this bath.

◄ THIS BATHROOM MIXES AND MATCHES traditional with modern, contrasting a claw-foot tub with a tall wall of slab-fronted cherry-veneer plywood doors and drawers. Flipper doors in the frameless cabinet fold back for unobstructed TV viewing.

▲ UNFITTED CABINETRY—in this case, a chest of drawers, a simple side table, and a floor-standing towel rack—fit in perfectly with the cottage-like feel of this bathroom.

◄ LOOKING MORE LIKE A LIBRARY than a bathroom, the floor-to-ceiling cherry cabinetry gives this retreat a quiet repose as well as plenty of practical storage space. The countertop drawers and the cabinets directly above them are located in the most easily accessed storage area, ideal for often-used items.

▶ DRAWING INSPIRATION from a smaller 1930s French buffet designed by Jean Michel Franck, this mahogany cabinet features sliding doors with reed opaque-glass panels and four small curio drawers above.

CABINET DOOR STYLES

Cabinets get their looks primarily from their door and drawer fronts. These basic door styles—and the numerous variations on them shown in the photographs in this book—are available for both frameless and face-frame cabinetry.

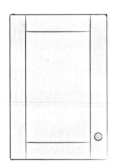

Frame and flat panel (or mirror)

Flat (or slab) door, usually in melamine or covered in laminate, with J-channel pull

Raised panel

Curved raised panel

Mullion glass panel (or mirror)

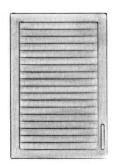

Ladder

Cathedral raised panel

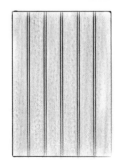

Board and batten

▶ WITH FOUR GENEROUS DRAWERS and a small cabinet in each, the two storage units flanking the open sink solve this bathroom's storage needs with style. The countertop and backsplash are made of Carrara marble, matching slabs cap the two cabinets and the tub deck.

◀ SOMETIMES OPEN SHELVING is the best storage solution, particularly in the case of this corner-mounted sink where a cabinet would be impractical.

VANITY OPTIONS

▼THE CLASSIC ELEGANCE of this master bathroom is matched by the formal look of the frame-and-panel doors and drawers on this double vanity.

◄WOVEN DOOR PANELS built with maple strips ventilate this tiger-maple vanity. It's topped with a custom-cast concrete countertop.

◄THE BEAUTIFULLY CURVED DOORS of this vanity give it a sculptural quality and conceal an ingenious assemblage of drawers and storage space. With its matching wooden countertop, this furniture-quality piece definitely doesn't belong in a bathroom for kids.

Cabinet and Door Hardware

L IKE A BADLY PLAYED MUSICAL FINALE, the wrong doorknobs and drawer pulls can leave your cabinetry looking flat. A seemingly small detail, cabinet hardware can have a big visual impact or can be chosen to be hardly no-ticeable at all. Match period cabinets with period-style knobs and pulls; check out building-salvage companies and flea markets for authentic antiques, as well as specialty stores and manufacturers who specialize in reproduction hardware.

Contemporary cabinetry gives you more design options, and in addition to the old standbys in porcelain and brass, you now can find pulls made of semiprecious stones, high-tech composites, and glass. Keep in mind, too, that knobs and pulls can have a big impact on the budget. While they typically start at a few dollars each, some can run $20 or more. If your bathroom has a lot of cabinetry, expensive hardware can end up costing several hundred dollars.

▲A SEEMINGLY SMALL DETAIL, cabinet hardware like these cast pewter turtle pulls can have a big impact on a bathroom's appearance—and budget.

▲ THIS DRESSERLIKE VANITY has been painted with an antique finish to match the muted earth tones in the marble countertop and faux marbleized walls.

▶ ELEGANTLY CARVED LEGS and a beautiful finish give this unfitted, custom-built mahogany vanity the look of fine furniture. The vanity is topped with a Rosa Verde granite countertop, the same stone found on the floor.

New Cabinets from Old Sources

WHEN IT COMES TO OUTFITTING YOUR BATHROOM with cabinetry, it pays to be creative. In fact, bathroom furniture can come from a wide variety of sources besides your local big-box building-supply store. Old bureaus, commodes, and tables suitable for conversion to bathroom use can be found almost anywhere—in flea markets or attics, at auctions or antique shops.

This dresser came from an attic and was originally covered with blue paint. While the dresser could have been stripped down to bare wood, it was instead selectively sanded to give it a distressed look. The drawer fronts were painted with a milk paint base, then "aged" by an application of antique crackle glaze. A final layer of buttermilk-colored milk paint gives the drawer fronts their textured alligator finish. Green latex paint protected by two layers of polyurethane varnish protects the top of the dresser.

To accommodate the plumbing, the drawer boxes were removed and the two lower drawer fronts attached together to make a door. The upper drawer front was reattached to the upper divider with hinges so that it would swing down, revealing his-and-her toothbrush holders attached to the inside of the drawer front. Inside, a pair of shelves provides plenty of storage area, while a small Kohler Boutique sink is shallow enough to fit the small space left at the top of the cabinet.

◀ WITH A LITTLE CREATIVITY and a new coat of "antique" paint, an old dresser finds new life as a character-filled vanity.

◀ WHAT WERE ONCE DRAWERS are now doors. The his-and-her toothbrush holders on the horizontally hinged upper door offer discrete storage.

THIS BUILT-IN VANITY features translucent tempered-glass doors that are frosted on the back side and mounted with the same type of hardware used for shower enclosures. The tile used on the floor and countertop is a synthetic composite terrazzo composed of quartz, marble, and sea glass with a resin binder.

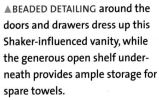

▲ BEADED DETAILING around the doors and drawers dress up this Shaker-influenced vanity, while the generous open shelf underneath provides ample storage for spare towels.

► OPEN SHELVES TAKE THE PLACE OF DRAWERS on this clear-grained fir vanity. Its sleek and uncluttered lines complement this contemporary bath.

Face Off

TIME WAS, there was a significant difference between the look of traditional face-frame cabinets and European-style frameless cabinets. While frameless cabinets shouted "contemporary," with their slab-type doors and decidedly modern pulls and hardware, traditional features, such as frame and panel doors, seemed to be exclusively reserved for face-frame cabinets.

The lines have blurred now, however, and it's possible to get frameless cabinets that have the same traditional look as face-frame cabinetry (see top photo). Frameless cabinets also offer a few advantages, such as slightly better accessibility to the interior of the cabinet (because there aren't any frames that reduce the size of the openings), heavier-duty cabinet boxes (because there is no face frame for reinforcement), and hardware that is more easily adjusted.

But just as frameless cabinets have co-opted some of the look of face-frame cabinets, many traditional cabinetmakers are adopting some of the features of frameless cabinetry. In particular, the hinge system that once gave frameless cabinetry such a decided advantage (because they're strong, hidden, and easily adjustable) has now been adapted to face-frame cabinetry (see bottom photo), and drawer slides for both types are now virtually identical.

◄FRAMELESS EUROPEAN-STYLE CABINETS offer slightly easier access to the interior than face-frame cabinets and are available in a wide range of finishes and styles.

◄FACE-FRAME CABINETS have a traditional look, and new European-style hinge systems allow their hardware to be concealed, an advantage once available only with frameless cabinetry.

MEDICINE CABINETS

▲SOMETIMES PLUMBING PIPES located directly behind a sink prohibit an inset medicine cabinet. The solution here was to mount a simple mirror above the sink and offset a more generous cabinet to the side.

▶LOOKING MORE LIKE A COLUMN than a cabinet, this curved-front medicine cabinet has carved and rounded detailing to match the organic look of this woodsy bathroom. The smaller cabinet at countertop level has sliding tambour doors that help it to blend in with the scenery.

▲ MUSEUM-GRADE PICTURE FRAMES fitted with beveled mirrors conceal these built-in medicine cabinets. The heavy frames are mounted with sturdy European-style cabinet hinges, which remain concealed when the doors are closed.

◄ THESE TALL, MIRRORED DOUBLE DOORS are held closed with a magnetic latch, and they open with a light touch.

Safety First

JUST BECAUSE A MEDICINE CABINET is placed over a sink, don't assume that it is inaccessible to children. The childproof containers that most prescription medicines are packaged in are a good deterrent, but they're not 100-percent effective (particularly when the caps aren't put back on completely). Many first-aid treatments, toiletries, and cleaning supplies are toxic as well. Play it safe: If there are small children around, place potentially dangerous items in a truly lockable medicine cabinet, and put childproof locks on cabinets that contain toxic cleaning supplies or other harmful materials.

OTHER CABINETRY & STORAGE

▶ SIMPLE FIR CABINETS suspended from the wall support a polished granite countertop and bowl-type sink, a configuration that opens up clear floor space underneath for wheelchair users.

▼ WHAT'S SO GREAT ABOUT SYMMETRY? Here, unusual stacked boxes echo the irregular tile pattern used on the walls of the bathroom, a theme repeated in the grids of the latticed cabinet doors. While it may look chaotic, there's a place for everything.

◀ THE OPEN SHELVING under this sink is reminiscent of Japanese *sunoko*, the traditional wooden slats found on the floors of Japanese baths. The mirror, countertop, towel bar, and shelving are all built from flamed redwood.

STORAGE GUIDELINES

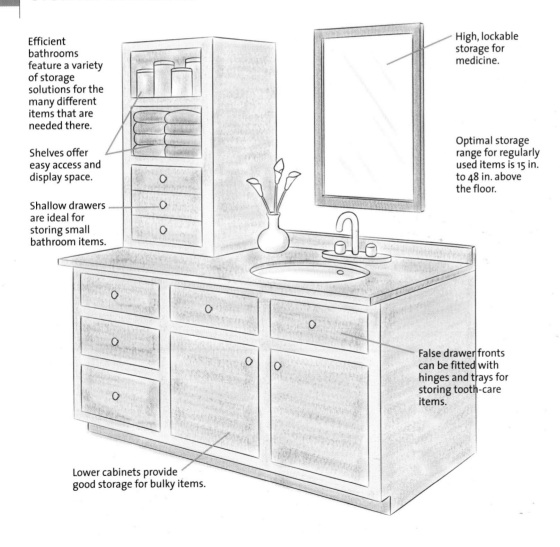

Efficient bathrooms feature a variety of storage solutions for the many different items that are needed there.

Shelves offer easy access and display space.

Shallow drawers are ideal for storing small bathroom items.

Lower cabinets provide good storage for bulky items.

High, lockable storage for medicine.

Optimal storage range for regularly used items is 15 in. to 48 in. above the floor.

False drawer fronts can be fitted with hinges and trays for storing tooth-care items.

▼THESE TALL TWIN CABINETS offer a storage alternative to conventional (and often cluttered) countertops, towel racks, and medicine cabinets.

▲A CASUAL AND PRACTICAL alternative to towel bars, these towel pegs don't take up as much space and are more user-friendly (and therefore more likely to be used).

▶EXCEPT FOR ITS CHEERFUL LIME-GREEN COLOR, this wheeled cart could be equally at home in a dentist's or doctor's office. Its good nature, water resistance, portability, and storage capacity would make it a perfect choice for a children's bathroom.

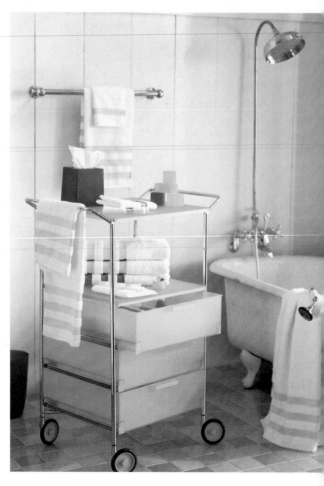

Creative Carpentry

SMALL BATHROOMS ARE USUALLY CRAMPED for space, and sometimes there is literally not enough room on the walls to hang enough towel racks. Sometimes a towel bar can be mounted underneath the window, particularly if the window is relatively small, as is often the case. But in this bathroom the window is large and extends below countertop height, which would have resulted in a placement that was too low to be practical.

The solution was to simply extend the window stool 3½ in. beyond the casing, which leaves enough room for a 2-in.-wide slot cut into the stool. Screws concealed by plugs at each end of the stool keep the ends from cracking at the weak points.

▲ THESE FOUR APOTHECARY-TYPE DRAWERS, lower central drawer, and upper shelves are located between knee and eye level—right where they're most easily reached. Save the bulky items that aren't frequently used for the more difficult-to-access cabinets below the sink.

▲ A SLOT CUT INTO THIS WINDOW stool turns it into a towel rack.

Shelving

Towels, perfume bottles, and many other items often found in a bathroom can be colorful and interesting to look at; shelves offer a way of displaying them instead of hiding them away.

Shallow shelves are generally more practical in a bathroom than deep shelves because items are less likely to get buried in back. If you have three or more shelves arranged vertically, making them adjustable will give you more flexibility in accommodating different-sized objects. Open shelves are perfect for displaying brightly colored bottles and soaps. One drawback: Shelves collect dust, so plan on using enclosed shelves for items that don't get used much.

▲ THIS MAHOGANY VANITY has a countertop-to-ceiling mirror, which helps to brighten the room and make it feel larger, but which also eliminates some of the room's storage possibilities. Here the flanking built-in open shelving helps make up for that lost storage space, and it's smartly located near the tub, where the towels will be needed most.

▲ A KNEEWALL CAN ADD AN INTERESTING architectural element to a room, but it also wastes potentially valuable floor space. These recessed storage cubbies take advantage of that unused area below a low ceiling, providing a convenient place for towels and bath items.

▶ IN THIS BATHROOM, a wall separates the bath from the toilet, giving both areas a degree of privacy. The trapezoidal opening framed into the wall is backed with a mirror and finished with glass shelves, helping to preserve that privacy while reflecting light from the nearby window back into the room.

◄EVEN THOUGH THIS BATHROOM IS LARGE, a solid cabinet of the same size would occupy a far larger visual "footprint" than this black-painted bamboo shelving unit. Because it isn't fixed to the wall, it can be easily moved to a new location if desired.

▲TOO OFTEN, SHOWERS ARE BUILT without adequate shelving or seating. Here, pie-shaped shelves discreetly tucked into the corner take up little room but hold the necessities, such as soap and shampoo.

Accessorize

BATHROOM STORAGE can be easily customized by adding one of a variety of different accessories now available. For example, plastic inserts that slip into standard-sized drawers help organize small objects like tooth-care products and cosmetics. A molded tray and special hinges can also be added to the false drawer fronts found on some vanities, a convenient place to store toothpaste and toothbrushes. There are also a variety of wire-basket add-ons, such as tilt-out and pull-out hampers and sliding trays for holding cleaning supplies.

Accessibility

As you look for bathroom hardware, keep in mind its function. Some knobs can be difficult to grasp, even for those with no physical disabilities, making it difficult—or even impossible for some—to open a door or drawer. In general, lever handles offer the most accessibility for latched doors, while D-shaped pulls are more accessible than knobs. Rule of thumb: The most accessible cabinet hardware can be operated using a closed fist.

▲TWO LENGTHS of picture-hanging wire strung between the two walls of this nook create instant storage for rolled up towels.

▶WITH PLENTY OF OPEN SHELVING in this bathroom, the need for under-sink storage was minimized and these stylish, suspended cabinets could be used in place of a traditional vanity. The overscale drawer pulls double as hand-towel bars.

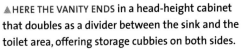

▲ HERE THE VANITY ENDS in a head-height cabinet that doubles as a divider between the sink and the toilet area, offering storage cubbies on both sides.

Lighting, Heating, and Ventilation

A window can be a bathroom's most important asset. Besides allowing sunlight and fresh air to stream in, a well-placed window can frame a great view, helping to bring the outdoors in both physically and psychologically. For all those other times when the sun doesn't shine you'll need to depend on good artificial sources for general illumination, task lighting, decorative lighting, and night-lighting.

Heat (and, in some climates, air-conditioning) is also an important component in any bathroom design. In general, a bathroom is more comfortable when it is about 5°F warmer than other rooms in the house. In some homes it's possible to add separate thermostatically controlled zones to control the temperature of each bathroom. When this isn't an option, there are a number of supplemental sources for heating and cooling a bathroom.

While the most environmentally friendly way to air out a bathroom is by opening a window, this isn't always practical in cold climates. While humid air may seem desirable in the dry winter months, high humidity can cause all sorts of problems, ranging from mold and mildew to rot in your home's structure. Bathrooms should be properly exhausted with a quiet, efficient, and properly sized ventilation system.

◄ INSTEAD OF A MIRROR, THIS VANITY has a dramatic round-top window in front of it to capture the light and frame the view. A smaller adjustable makeup mirror serves both the sink and the seating area, which has task lighting supplied by two wall-mounted sconces. Slatted wooden enclosures at either end of the vanity conceal old-fashioned cast-iron radiators while still allowing warm air to circulate around the room.

A Look at Lighting

WINDOWS LET IN LIGHT and keep us connected with the outside world. Choose a specific window type—casement or double-hung, for example—for the way it matches your home's architecture. But orient your windows so that they take best advantage of the available view without compromising privacy within.

When the sun goes down and you turn on the lights, you should like what you see. Choose lighting fixtures that provide both general illumination and good task lighting for activities such as applying cosmetics or shaving. Accent and decorative lighting can be used to add an element of drama, while suitable controls, such as timers and dimmers, can be used to create just the right mood.

▲ FOR BATHROOMS THAT ARE TUCKED INTO odd spaces, a skylight can be an excellent source of natural light that also provides ventilation if it's operable.

◀ WITH THREE FIXED-SASH windows located high on the wall for both natural light and privacy and two smaller operable awning windows below for ventilation, this tub alcove is bright but not exposed. A panel radiator mounted on the far wall warms the space with gentle even heat and helps dry out towels.

◀ WHERE PRIVACY ISN'T AN ISSUE, this floor-to-ceiling glass panel behind the vanity is a stunning alternative to a wall and literally brings the outdoors inside. Attaching a simple mirror to the middle of the panel creates the impression that it's floating above the sink.

▼ A VAULTED CEILING with a sizable skylight, large windows over the tub, and the generous mirror over the sink, make this bathroom feel spacious despite its small size. While not as desirable as light fixtures placed at eye level on either side of the sink, the theater-style lighting over the mirror is a good alternative that provides even, illumination of the vanity.

NATURAL LIGHTING

▲▲ A SKYLIGHT IS A GREAT WAY to dramatically transform an interior space and flood it with natural light, but avoid placing it directly over the tub if you live in a cold climate. Skylights create a cool draft because of the convection loop that forms as warm air rises and then cools as it hits the cold surface of the window glass.

◀ IMAGINE HOW CRAMPED this master bath would feel without the dramatic skylight, which adds volume and light to the room. White wainscoting and brightly finished wall surfaces help keep the room cheerful.

◄ MINIMALLY SEPARATED FROM THE OUTDOORS by a frameless glass enclosure, this soaking tub is almost a part of the private garden. The shower adjacent to the tub has a door opening directly to the garden, creating the feeling of an outdoor bath in an indoor space.

Window Basics

CHOOSING APPROPRIATE WINDOWS for your bathroom is part art and part science. Most of the time we buy a particular type of window—double-hung, casement, awning, etc.—based on its looks and a home's architectural style. But when you consider the fact that 30 percent of the average home's heating or air-conditioning dollars are lost out the windows, it pays to consider a window's energy efficiency too.

Besides improved frames and sashes that conduct less heat and cut down on air infiltration, the biggest improvements in windows lately are the new low-e coatings and gas fills used on insulated double-pane window glass. Low-e coatings are virtually invisible and are applied to one of the inner surfaces of insulated glass. They help control the amount of solar energy that passes into a room and reduce the amount of radiated heat leaving a room. Gas fills—typically argon or krypton—are used instead of air inside the two layers of insulated glass, further decreasing the amount of heat conducted through a window.

Most windows are now labeled by the National Fenestration Rating Council (NFRC), providing a way to compare the true energy performance of different windows. The label is also a good guide for determining the best window for your particular climate and application.

▲THIS WINDOW COMPOSITION pays playful homage to the original faceted triangular windows found in the attic gables of this historic Greek Revival house. Though it lets in plenty of light, this configuration also reserves a degree of privacy, especially when the blinds are drawn.

▲BESIDES PROVIDING A GREAT VIEW of the nearby Atlantic Ocean, these crank-operated casement windows swing out wide to provide 100-percent ventilation. They provide abundant natural light to the bathroom, which is supplemented by recessed lighting overhead that illuminates a honed black-slate countertop and hammered-nickel sinks.

◀ANOTHER FACTOR TO CONSIDER when locating a skylight is exposure to the sun. In a warm climate, a skylight with southern, western, or southwestern exposure will overheat the room, especially a skylight that is as large as this. A skylight with eastern exposure will get morning sun, while a skylight with northern exposure will provide more diffuse light and little solar gain all day long.

Brightening Up a Shower

A SHOWER CAN BE DARK AND GLOOMY, at least when the lights are off. To make them brighter and more cheerful, architect Keith Moskow likes to install a window right in the shower stall. Though he typically installs the window in an exterior wall for the view, in his own bathroom he installed a small round window in an interior partition wall.

To avoid water damage, the window is placed high on the wall and is reversed so that the exterior side is facing the inside of the shower. Besides the fixed round window shown here, Moskow has had good luck using casement windows with their sills reconfigured so that they have a pitch to drain water. He also recommends using exterior-grade paint and/or clear varnish to protect any wood surfaces.

◀BESIDES ADDING an interesting architectural touch, this circular window brightens up the shower enclosure with light from the adjacent bathroom.

ARTIFICIAL LIGHTING

▶ MOST OF THIS MASTER BATH'S general lighting is supplied by a suspended uplight fixture that directs incandescent light up toward the ceiling, where it is reflected back into the room for subdued but effective lighting.

▼ HIDDEN BEHIND THIS MIRROR are a pair of linear fluorescent lights, which are mounted in the 4-in. space between the mirror and the wall behind it. Light bounces off the back of the mirror and turns the glass block wall into a luminous surface.

▲ THE PAIR OF PLEATED FIXTURES that flanks this classically trimmed mirror provides even, shadow-free lighting at the vanity.

Making the Most of Mirrors

I T'S THE RARE BATHROOM THAT doesn't have at least one mirror, usually mounted right above the sink. But besides offering the chance to check our own appearance, mirrors can have a dramatic impact on a bathroom's appearance that's way out of proportion to their modest cost.

When mounted on the long wall of a narrow bathroom, for example, a large mirror can give the room the sense of increased depth and spaciousness. Multiple mirrors can be used as an architectural element, creating a changing panorama of complex images that can make a simple rectangular room far more interesting (see top photo). If there is a window nearby, a mirror can make a bath feel brighter by reflecting ambient light all around the room (see bottom photo).

There are a number of ways to install mirrors in a bathroom. A glass shop can supply mirrors in almost any size and shape; these glass panels are then attached directly to the wall with a proprietary mastic, often without any visible frame. The supplier can also drill holes in the glass for mounting light or plumbing fixtures.

Alternately, mirrors can be mounted in frames that can be fixed to a wall or attached to adjustable arms. They can be used as cabinet doors (either with or without frames), or as tub and shower doors. Like glass, mirrors can be etched or sandblasted with designs or given beveled edges.

◄ FINISHED IN MARBLE AND MIRROR MOSAICS, this small powder room is a study in texture and light.

▲ A CUSTOM DESIGN sandblasted into the mirrors surrounding this tub alcove give the space depth and complexity.

►THIS HIGH-CEILINGED LOFT has a fantastic wall-to-wall window that floods the room with natural light, which is supplemented by fixtures suspended from the ceiling.

Designing Bathroom Lighting

IN ADDITION TO ABUNDANT NATURAL LIGHT, bathrooms should have good general (or ambient) lighting and task lighting, typically the lighting found around the vanity area. In small bathrooms, general and task lighting can often be combined, while in larger bathrooms, specific areas, such as the shower, the toilet, the sink, and the tub, will each require appropriate task lighting.

At the vanity, the best type of illumination is provided by a pair of fixtures mounted at eye level on either side of the mirror, a configuration that evenly and naturally lights up the face. The worst kind of illumination is provided by a ceiling-mounted fixture over the sink, or by a fixture placed over the mirror, because this kind of light casts shadows downward. It's important to remember that the goal of vanity lighting is not to light the mirror, the sink, or the top of the head, but to light the face.

In general, try to choose lamps and fixtures that will give you the most natural-looking and energy-efficient lighting. Dimmers are also a good idea, allowing you to control the light level in specific parts of your bathroom. If you're feeling adventurous, think about adding accent and decorative lighting, which can create unique effects in your bathroom.

▲WHILE THE LARGE ROUND WINDOW is a great source of natural light, the two fixtures mounted at eye level on either side of the mirror above the sink is the best configuration for task lighting, providing a flattering, shadow-free, vertical cross-illumination.

◄ COLOR-CORRECTED LINEAR fluorescent fixtures provide the kind of shadow-free task lighting that is matched in quality only by the natural light that enters the room from the large window reflected in these mirrors.

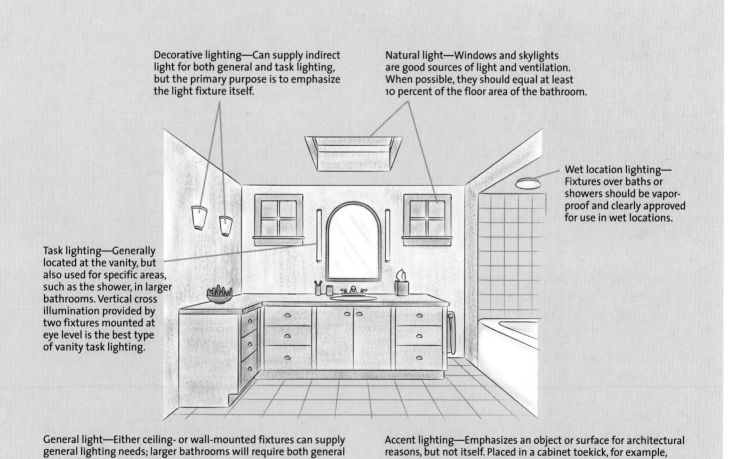

Decorative lighting—Can supply indirect light for both general and task lighting, but the primary purpose is to emphasize the light fixture itself.

Natural light—Windows and skylights are good sources of light and ventilation. When possible, they should equal at least 10 percent of the floor area of the bathroom.

Wet location lighting—Fixtures over baths or showers should be vapor-proof and clearly approved for use in wet locations.

Task lighting—Generally located at the vanity, but also used for specific areas, such as the shower, in larger bathrooms. Vertical cross illumination provided by two fixtures mounted at eye level is the best type of vanity task lighting.

General light—Either ceiling- or wall-mounted fixtures can supply general lighting needs; larger bathrooms will require both general and task lighting. Plan on about 1 watt of incandescent light per sq. ft. of floor area for ceiling-mounted fixtures, twice that amount for recessed fixtures, and one-third to one-half that amount for fluorescent fixtures.

Accent lighting—Emphasizes an object or surface for architectural reasons, but not itself. Placed in a cabinet toekick, for example, accent lighting can make the vanity appear to float while also functioning as effective night lighting.

Climate Control

WHEN THE TEMPERATURE, WIND, AND HUMIDITY ARE JUST RIGHT, we feel comfortable. This is the "comfort zone," and while it varies a bit from individual to individual, humans require a relatively narrowly defined combination of heat, relative humidity, and air circulation in order to feel neither too hot nor too cold. In the bathroom, our comfort zone is usually about 5°F higher than in the rest of the house, simply because we usually wear less clothing there.

Bathrooms have a comfort zone too: Quite simply, too much heat and humidity will rot a bathroom from the inside out. This is why a reliable, efficient, and foolproof ventilation system is indispensable.

▼SOME CAST-IRON RADIATORS can be spruced up simply with a new coat of paint, but a custom wooden radiator cover is another option that can cover up serious flaws while providing useful shelf storage.

◀ BATHROOMS WILL REQUIRE ground-fault protection, like the GFCI outlet shown here. Instead of the cheap plastic cover plates that come with most outlets and switches, consider using stainless-steel cover plates, which look better and can be selected to match the other accessories in your bathroom.

All About Ventilation

HIGH HUMIDITY LEVELS in a bathroom can cause all sorts of problems, ranging from condensation on the mirrors and peeling wallpaper to mildew, mold, and rot. That's why a good ventilation system—not just an operable window—is a must in any bathroom. The heart of the system is the fan, which moves humid air out from the bathroom through a duct, from which it is exhausted outside.

Bathroom fans are rated according to the volume of air they can move in cubic feet per minute (cfm) and by their noise level (in sones). A small 5-ft. by 9-ft. bathroom requires a fan capable of moving 50 cfm, while a larger bathroom may need a 90-cfm or 150-cfm fan. Steer clear of fans that have sone ratings higher than 3; they're too loud.

The best fans are rated at around 1 sone (about the same amount of noise produced by a refrigerator humming in a kitchen) and are barely audible.

Most fans are operated by a simple switch, but they can also be put on timers, which ensures that the fan is turned off when the air is cleared of excess humidity (a good feature for very quiet fans). Another option is a humidistat control that turns the fan on automatically whenever humidity levels are high.

▶ A BATHROOM FAN DOESN'T DO ANY GOOD if it isn't used. When this fan-delay timer switch is flipped on, both the bathroom light and ventilation fan turn on, but when you switch the light off the fan keeps on running on an adjustable timer for up to 60 minutes, giving the fan time to exhaust moisture and odors.

▲ WHAT'S MORE ROMANTIC than a bath by firelight? This three-sided, gas-fueled fireplace provides extra warmth and also serves as a divider between the bath area and adjacent master bedroom.

Electric Mirror Defogger

UNLESS YOUR BATHROOM IS EXTREMELY WARM and your ventilation system extremely powerful, your mirrors will fog whenever you take a shower or bath. Several companies offer solutions that will keep at least a portion of your mirror fog-free. For example, Electric Mirror is a heater configured as a mat that is mounted behind a mirror and wired into an electric box. When the heater is on, the mirror stays warm and fog-free, even in the steamiest bathroom.

Heating Options

I F YOU'VE GOT A COLD BATHROOM, there are a number of options for heating it up. The simplest solution is a stand-alone, electrically powered heater that mounts on a ceiling, a wall, or in the kickspace below a vanity cabinet. For example, an infrared heat lamp or a ceiling-mounted forced-air heater might provide enough extra heat to make a cool bathroom comfortable.

If you need more heat, a better option might be a wall-mounted electric heater with a fan to put heat right where it's needed most—at floor level. For the ultimate in comfort, though, consider a radiant system. These can be powered by electricity or by an existing hot-water heating system and typically consist of tubes or coils buried in the floor, walls, or ceiling of your bathroom. Invisible, silent, and draft free, a radiant heating system can turn a cold tile floor into a warm radiator.

▲ IT'S THE FINISHING TOUCHES—here, reproduction push-button light switches with a brass cover plate—that give a period bath an authentic look.

▲ MOST EXHAUST FANS have a plastic cover that can look out of place in many bathrooms. Architect David Edrington replaces his with metal grates, in this case an antique wall register that was plated to match the other fixtures in the bathroom. In some cases, Edrington mounts a small wood frame to the ceiling first to provide clearance for the light fixtures that are in some exhaust fans; the metal grill is then screwed to the frame.

▲ THIS ELECTRICALLY POWERED PANEL RADIATOR is an excellent supplementary heat source that's easily mountable on any wall, right where it's needed most. It doubles as a towel warmer.

Resources

American Fiber Cement
Corporation
6901 S. Pierce St.,
Suite 260 Littleton, CO 80128
800-688-8677
www.AmericanFiberCement.com

Americh Corp.
10700 John Price Rd.
Charlotte, NC 28273
800-453-1463
www.americh.com

Ann Sacks Tile & Stone, Inc.
8120 N.E. 33rd Dr.
Portland, OR 97211
800-278-8453
www.annsacks.com

Arjo Inc.
50 N. Gary Ave.
Roselle, IL 60172
800-323-1245
www.arjo.com

Avonite, Inc.
1945 Highway 304
Belen, NM 87002
800-428-6648
www.avonite.com

Briggs Plumbing Products, Inc.
P.O. Box 71077
Charleston, SC 29415
800-888-4458
www.briggsplumbing.com

CaesarStone
Sdot-Yam
38805 M.P. Menashe
Israel
+972-4-6261267
www.caesarstone.com

Clivus Multrum
15 Union St.
Lawrence, MA 01840
800-425-4887
www.clivusmultrum.com

Cosentino USA, Inc.
(Silestone)
10707 Corporate Dr.,
Suite 136 Stafford, TX 77477
281-494-7277
www.silestoneusa.com

CTT Furniture
(water-resistant
acrylic-modified paper)
7034 Carroll Rd.
San Diego, CA 92121
858-587-9311
www.cttfurniture.com

Dornbracht USA
1700 Executive Dr., Suite 600
Duluth, GA 30096
800-774-1181
www.dornbracht.com

DuPont Surfaces
(Corian, Zodiaq)
4417 Lancaster Pike
Wilmington, DE 19805
800-426-7426
www.corian.com

DURAVIT USA, Inc.
1750 Breckinridge Pwy.,
Suite 500
Duluth, GA 30096
888-387-2848
www.duravit.com

Electric Mirror, Inc.
P.O. Box 2426
Lynnwood, WA 98036-2426
888-218-9238
www.electricmirror.com

Endless Pools, Inc.
200 East Dutton Mill Rd.
Aston, PA 19014
800-732-8660
www.endlesspools.com

Energy Federation Inc.
40 Washington St.
Westborough, MA 01581
800-876-0660
www.efi.org

Fireslate
3065 Cranberry Hwy.,
Unit 24A
E. Wareham, MA 02538
800-523-5902
www.fireslate.com

Formica Corporation
(Surell)
15 Independence Blvd.
Warren, NJ 07059
800-367-6422
www.formica.com

FST/Y-Slip USA Corporation
2077 Sunnydale Blvd.
Clearwater, FL 33765
888-949-7547
www.y-slip.com

Imperial Home Decor Group
(Anaglypta)
23645 Mercantile Rd.
Cleveland, OH 44122
888-608-5943
www.ihdg.com

Jacuzzi Whirlpool Bath
2121 N. California Blvd.,
Suite 475
Walnut Creek, CA 94596
925-938-7070
www.jacuzzi.com

Kohler Plumbing
444 Highland Dr.
Kohler, WI 53044
800-456-4537
www.kohler.com

Luxury Bath Systems
Luxury Bath Liners, Inc.
232 James Ct.
Bensenville, IL 60106
800-822-7905

National Kitchen and Bath
Association (NKBA)
687 Willow Grove St.
Hackettstown, NJ 07840
800-843-6522
www.nkba.org

ROMA Steam Bath Inc.
16802 Barker Spring Rd.,
Suite 500
Houston, TX 77084-5505
800-657-0656
www.Romasteambath.com

Runtal® North America, Inc.
187 Neck Rd.
P.O. Box 8278
Ward Hill, MA 01835
800-526-2621
www.runtalnorthamerica.com

Swan Corporation
(Swanstone™)
One City Centre, Suite 2300
St. Louis, MO 63101
800-325-7008
www.theswancorp.com

Syndesis Studio, Inc.
(Syndecrete)
2908 Colorado Ave.
Santa Monica, CA 90403-3616
310-829-9932
www.syndesisinc.com

Toto USA, Inc.
1155 Southern Rd.
Morrow, GA 30260
800-350-8686
www.totousa.com

Trespa North America Ltd.
800-4-TRESPA
www.trespanorthamerica.com

Vola A/S
Lunavej 2
DK-8700 Horsens
Denmark
+45-7023-5500
www.vola.dk

Wilsonart International
(Gibraltar®, Earthstone™)
P.O. Box 6110
Temple, TX 76503-6110
800-433-3222
www.wilsonart.com

Credits

CHAPTER: 1

p. 4: Photo: © Brian VandenBrink, Photographer 2003; Design: Weston Hewitson Architects Inc., Hingham, MA

p. 6: (left) Photo: © 2003 carolynbates.com, courtesy the Shelburne Museum, Shelburne, VT; (right) Photo: © Peter Bastianelli-Kerze; Design: Dale Mulfinger and Steven Buetow, SALA Architects, Minneapolis, MN

p. 7: (top) Photo: © Tim Street-Porter; Design: Carol Beth Cozen, Cozen Architecture, Manhattan Beach, CA ; (bottom) Photo: © Brian VandenBrink, Photographer 2003; Design: Atlantic Kitchen Center, Portland, ME

p. 8: Photo: © Mark Samu, courtesy Benjamin Moore & Co., Montvale, NJ

p. 9: (left) Photo: Charles Bickford, © The Taunton Press, Inc.; Design: Patrick Camus, Alexandria, VA; (right) Photo: Kevin Ireton, © The Taunton Press, Inc.; Design: Goforth-Gill Architects, Seattle, WA

p. 10: (left) Photo: © National Kitchen & Bath Association, photo by Bill LaFevor; Design: Terry Burton, Hermitage Kitchen & Bath Gallery, Nashville, TN; (right) Photo: © National Kitchen & Bath Association, photo by Kaskel Architectural; Design: Connie Schey, Insignia Kitchen & Bath Design Group Ltd., Barrington, IL

p. 11: (top) Photo: Charles Bickford, © The Taunton Press, Inc.; Design: John T. Conroy, Princeton, NJ; (bottom) Charles Bickford, © The Taunton Press, Inc.; Design: John T. Conroy, Princeton, NJ

p. 12: Photo: © National Kitchen & Bath Association, photo by Peter Leach; Design: Sandra Steiner-Houck, CKD, Mechanicsburg, PA

p. 13: (left) Photo: Tom O'Brien; Design: Louis A. DiBerardino, New Canaan, CT; (right) Photo: © National Kitchen & Bath Association, photo by Miguel Hortiguela; Design: Tim Scott/Erica Westeroth, XTC Designs Inc., Toronto, Ontario, Canada

p. 14: (left) Photo: © Brian VandenBrink, Photographer 2003; Design: Weston Hewitson Architects Inc., Hingham, MA; (top & bottom right) Photo: Charles Miller, © The Taunton Press, Inc.; Design: Steven Vanze/Barnes Vanze, Washington, DC

p. 15: Photo: © Brian VandenBrink, Photographer 2003; Design: Mark Hutker Associates, Martha's Vineyard, MA

p. 16: Photo: © National Kitchen & Bath Association, photo by Philip Fredericks; Design: Merrie Fredericks, Selective Design and Construction, Landsdowne, PA

p. 17: (top) Photo: © Brian VandenBrink, Photographer 2003; Design: Atlantic Kitchen Center, Portland, ME; (bottom) Photo: Charles Miller, © The Taunton Press, Inc.; Design: Sheryl Murray-Hansen/ Renovation Innovations, Portland, OR

p. 18: Photos: © Peter Malinowski/ Insite; Tile: Michelle Griffoul, Buellton, CA

p. 19: Photos: David Ericson; Design: Paul Bialowas, Ardsley, NY

p. 20: (left) Photo: © davidduncanlivingston.com; Design: Kendall Wilkinson Design/Patina Atelier, San Francisco, CA; (right) Photo: © National Kitchen & Bath Association, photo by Miguel Hortiguela; Design: Erica Westeroth/Tim Scott, XTC Designs Inc., Toronto, Ontario, Canada

p. 21: (left) © National Kitchen & Bath Association, photo by Miguel Hortiguela; Design: Erica Westeroth/Tim Scott, XTC Designs Inc., Toronto, Ontario, Canada; (right) Photo: © Jeremy Samuelson

p. 22: Photos: Charles Miller, © The Taunton Press, Inc.; Design: David Edrington, Eugene, OR

p. 23: Photos: Charles Miller, © The Taunton Press, Inc.; Design: David Edrington, Eugene, OR

p. 25: Photo: David Ericson; Design: Dennis Parker, Honolulu, HI

p. 26: Photo: © Brian VandenBrink, Photographer 2003; Design: Donham & Sweeney Architects, Boston, MA

p. 27: Photo: Charles Miller, © The Taunton Press, Inc.; Design: Helen Degenhardt, Berkeley, CA

p. 28: Photo: ©Tim Street-Porter; Design: Suzanne Rheinstein, Hollywood, CA

p. 29: (left) Photo: © davidduncanlivingston.com; (right) Photo: Charles Bickford, © The Taunton Press, Inc.; Design: Sarah Susanka, Raleigh, NC

p. 30: (top) © National Kitchen & Bath Association, photo by Hawks Photography, Inc.; Design: Alan Hilsabeck Jr., The Great Indoors, Farmer's Branch, TX; (bottom) Photo: © davidduncanlivingston.com

p. 31: (top) Photo: © davidduncanlivingston.com; (bottom) Photo: © 2003 carolynbates.com; Design: Brad Rabinowitz, Burlington, VT

p. 32: Photo: © Brian VandenBrink, Photographer 2003; Tile: Rob Romano, Brunswick, ME; General Contractor: Axel Berg, Falmouth, ME

p. 33: (left) Photo: © 2003 carolynbates.com; Design: Patrick Kane/Black River Design, Montpelier, VT; (right) Photo: © 2003 carolynbates.com; Design: Cushman & Beckstrom, Inc. Architecture and Planning, Stowe, VT

CHAPTER: 2

p. 34: Photo: © Jeremy Samuelson

p. 36: (top) © Mark Samu; Design: Ellen Roche Architects, Oyster Bay, NY; (bottom) Photo: © Brian VandenBrink, Photographer 2003; Design: Dominic Paul Mercadante Architecture, Belfast, ME

p. 37: (left) Photo: ©Tim Street-Porter; Design: Steven Ehrlich Architects, Culver City, CA; (right) Photo: Charles Bickford, © The Taunton Press, Inc.; Design: David Sellers, Warren, VT

p. 38: Photos: Roe A. Osborn, © The Taunton Press, Inc.; Design: Jack Burnett-Stuart and Julia Strickland, Los Angeles, CA

p. 39: (left) Photo: Kevin Ireton, © The Taunton Press, Inc.; Design: Tom Vermeland, Minneapolis, MN.; (right) Photo: Scott Gibson, © The Taunton Press, Inc.; Design: Sam Hill, Nantucket, MA

p. 40: Photos: Roe A. Osborn, © The Taunton Press, Inc.; Design: Pete and Connie Di Girolamo, San Diego, CA; Builder: Glen Stewart

p. 41: (left top) Photo: Roe A. Osborn, © The Taunton Press, Inc.; Design: Laura Du Charme Conboy, La Jolla, CA; (left) Photo: Charles Miller, © The Taunton Press, Inc.; Design: Bentley & Churchill, Architects, Siasconset, Nantucket, MA; Builder: Michael Phillips Construction, Nantucket, MA; (right) Photo: © 2003 carolynbates.com; Design: Joan Shannon, Burlington, VT

p. 42: Photo: Roe A. Osborn, © The Taunton Press, Inc.; Design: William Rennie Boyd, Santa Cruz, CA

p. 43: Photo: Charles Bickford, © The Taunton Press, Inc.; Design: Marcia Wake, ME

p. 44: (left) Photo: © Tim Street-Porter; Design: Fung + Blatt Architects, Los Angeles, CA; (top right) Photo: © Tim Street-Porter; Design: Hagy Belzberg Architects, Santa Monica, CA ; (bottom right) Photo: © Jeremy Samuelson; Design: Jennifer Luce, La Jolla, CA

p. 45: Photo: © Brian VandenBrink, Photographer 2003; Design: William Winkelman with Whitten Architects, Portland, ME

p. 46: Photo: © Brian VandenBrink, Photographer 2003; Design: Pete and Paula Stone Tile Design, Salida, CO

p. 47: (right) Photo: © Roger Turk/Northlight Photography, Inc.; Design: Becky Kelleran/The Showplace Inc., Redmond, WA; (left) Photo: Charles Miller, © The Taunton Press, Inc.; Design: Diane Kushner, San Miguel de Allende, Mexico

p. 48: (left) Photo © Mark Samu, courtesy of Hearst Special; (right) Photo: Charles Bickford, © The Taunton Press, Inc.; Tile: Pat Wehrman/Dodge Lane Pottery Group, Sonora, CA

p. 49: (left & right) Photo: Kevin Ireton, © The Taunton Press, Inc.; Design: Noel Norskog, Santa Fe, NM; Builder: Steve Bone, Santa Fe, NM; Tile: Michael Coon, Santa Fe, NM

p. 50: (top) Photo: © Tim Street-Porter; Design: Marmol Radzinger + Associates, Santa Monica, CA; (bottom) Photo: © davidduncanlivingston.com

p. 51: (left top) Photo: © Brian Vanden Brink, Photographer 2003; Design: Weston Hewitson Architects Inc., Hingham, MA; (right) Photo: Charles Miller, © The Taunton Press, Inc.; (left bottom) Photo: Scott Phillips, © The Taunton Press, Inc.

p. 52: (left) Photo: © Mark Samu; Design: Daniel Barsanti/Healing Barsanti, Inc., New York, NY; (right) Photo: ©Brian Vanden Brink, Photographer 2003

p. 53: (top & bottom) Photo: Charles Miller, © The Taunton Press, Inc.; Design: Dan Allen, Seattle, WA; (right) Photo: © Hester & Hardaway; Design:Sharon Tyler Hoover; Builder: Perales Cabinet Shop, Del Valle, TX

p. 54: (left) Photo: © davidduncanlivingston.com; Design: Lamperti Associates, San Rafael, CA; (top right) Photo: © Jeremy Samuelson; Design: Jennifer Luce, La Jolla, CA; (bottom right) Photo: © Mark Samu; Design: Lee Najman Interiors, Port Washington, NY

p. 55: (left top) Photo: © Tim Street-Porter; (left bottom) Photo: © 2003 carolynbates.com;. Design: Ted Montgomery, Indiana Architecture, Charlotte, VT; (right) Photo: Scott Phillips, © The Taunton Press, Inc.

p. 56: (left) Photo: © davidduncanlivingston.com.; (right) Photo: Charles Bickford, © The Taunton Press, Inc.; Design: David Hert/Syndesis Inc., Santa Monica, CA

p. 57: (left top) Photo: Charles Miller, © The Taunton Press, Inc.; Design: House + House, San Francisco, CA; (left bottom) Photo: Charles Bickford, © The Taunton Press, Inc.; Design: Dan Rockhill, Lawrence, KS; (right) Photo: © Van Noy Photography; Design: Ronald E. Cox, Napa, CA

p. 58: (top) Photo: © Tim Street-Porter; (bottom) Photo byLarry Falke; Design by Gary White, Kitchen & Bath Design, Newport Beach, CA

p. 59: Photo: © 2003 carolynbates.com; Design: Gary Crowley, Colchester, VT

p. 60: (left) Photo: © davidduncanlivingston.com; (top right) Photo: Scott Phillips, © The Taunton Press, Inc.; (bottom right) Photo: © Jeremy Samuelson

p. 61: (top) Photo: © Mark Samu, courtesy of Hearst Specials; (bottom) Photo: Scott Phillips, © The Taunton Press, Inc.

p. 62 (left & right) Photos: Charles Bickford, © The Taunton Press, Inc.; Design: Dale Brentrup, Charlotte, NC

p. 63: (left) Photo: © Mark Samu, courtesy of Hearst Specials;(right) © Brian VandenBrink, Photographer 2003; Design: William Winkelman with Whitten Architects, Portland, ME

p. 64: (top) Photo: Scott Phillips, © The Taunton Press, Inc.; (bottom) Photo Courtesy of Formica Corporation

p. 65: Photo Courtesy of Formica Corporation

p. 66: (left & right) Photos: Andy Engel, © The Taunton Press, Inc.; Design: Guy N. Grassi, Boston, MA

p. 67: (left top) Photo: © Brian VandenBrink, Photographer 2003; Design: Quinn Evans/Architects, Washington, DC/Ann Arbor, MI; (left bottom) Photo: ©Steve Vierra; Design: Loraine McKenna, Duxbury, MA; (right) Photo: Charles Bickford, © The Taunton Press, Inc.; Designer: John Siebert, Birdseye Building Company, Richmond, VT

CHAPTER: 3

p. 68: Photo: © Brian VandenBrink, Photographer 2003; Design: Mark Hutker & Associates, Architects, Inc., Vineyard Haven, MA

p. 70: (top) Photo: © Brian VandenBrink, Photographer 2003; (bottom) Photo: © Tim Street-Porter

p. 71: (top) Photo: © Tim Street-Porter; Design: Tracy Murdock Design Studio, Los Angeles, CA ; (bottom) Photo & Design: Richard Brewster, Cutchogue, NY

p. 72: (left) Photo: Charles Bickford, © The Taunton Press, Inc.; Design: Leslie Hill/Jim Kirby, Brookline, VT; (top right) Photo: © Tim Street-Porter; Design: Tracy Murdock Design Studio, Los Angeles, CA; (bottom left) Photo: Charles Bickford, © The Taunton Press, Inc.; Design: Ron DiMauro; Builder: Glenn Sherman, RI

p. 73: (top) Photo: © 2003 carolyn-bates.com; Design: Cushman & Beckstrom, Inc., Architecture and Planning, Stowe, VT; (bottom) Photo: © Brian VandenBrink, Photographer 2003

p. 74: (left) Photo: © Tim Street-Porter; Design: Duccio Ermenegildo, Mexico; (right) © Brian VandenBrink, Photographer 2003; Design: Mike Homer, Falmouth, ME

p. 75: (top) Photo: © Steve Vierra; Design: Anthony Catalfano Interiors, Inc., Boston, MA; Builder: Woodmeister Corp., Worcester, MA; (bottom) Photo courtesy of Arjo Inc.

p. 76: (top) Photo: © Steve Vierra; Builder: Wellen Construction, Marlborough, MA; (bottom) Photo: © Tim Street-Porter; Design: Duccio Ermenegildo, Mexico

p. 77: (top) Photo: © Tim Street-Porter; (bottom left) Photo: Charles Miller, © The Taunton Press, Inc.; Design: Bentley & Churchill, Architects, Siasconset, Nantucket, MA; Builder: Michael Phillips Construction, Nantucket, MA; (bottom right) Photo: © Mark Samu; Design: Sherrill Canet Interiors Ltd., New York, NY

p. 78: (top) Photo: Charles Miller, © The Taunton Press, Inc.; Design: Steven Vanze/Barnes Vanze, Washington, DC; (bottom) Photo: Scott Gibson, © The Taunton Press, Inc.

p. 79: Photos: © Grey Crawford; Designer & Builder: Jim Garramone, Evanston, IL

p. 80: (left) Photo: © Bruce T. Martin 2003; Design: Kennedy & Violich Architecture, MA; Builder: Kistler and Knapp Builders, Acton, MA; (top right) Photo: © David Glomb; Design: Steve Badanes/Jersey Devil; (bottom right) Photo: © Steve Vierra; Design: Delight Nelson-Gelinas/Interiors Delight, Merrimack, NH

p. 81: (top) Photo: © davidduncanliv-ingston.com; (bottom) Photo courtesy of Endless Pools, Inc.

p. 82: (left) Photo Andy Engel, © The Taunton Press, Inc.; Design: Brendan Coburn, Brooklyn, NY ; (right) Photo: © Mark Ashley; Design: Patina Design Architects, Bainbridge Island, WA

p. 83: © 2003 carolynbates.com; Design: Cushman & Beckstrom, Inc., Architecture and Planning, Stowe, VT; (right) Photo: © Mark Samu, courtesy Hearst Specials

p. 84: (top) Photo: © davidduncanliving-ston.com; (bottom) Photo: Photo courtesy of Kohler Co.

p. 85: Photos: Scott Gibson, © The Taunton Press, Inc.

p. 86: (left) Photo: © Claudio Santini Photographer, www.claudiosantini.com; Design: House + House Architects, San Francisco, CA; (right) © Brian VandenBrink, Photographer 2003;m Design: Bruce Norelius, Elliott & Elliott Architecture, Blue Hill, ME

p. 87: Photo: © Ken Gutmaker; Design: Linder Jones; Builder: Harrell Remodeling, Mountainview, CA

p. 88: Photo: © Brian VandenBrink, Photographer 2003; Design: Morningstar Marble & Granite, Inc., Topsham, ME

p. 89: (top) Photo: Charles Miller, © The Taunton Press, Inc.; Design: Stephen Vanze/Barnes Vanze, Washington, DC; (bottom) Photo: Steve Vierra; Design, Builder: Wellen Construction, Marlborough, MA

pp. 90-91: (left) Photos: Andy Engel, © The Taunton Press, Inc.

p. 92: (top) Photo: © Jeremy Samuelson; Design: Jim Lord and Bobby Dent, The Comfort Common, Comfort, TX; (bottom) Photo: © Jeremy Samuelson; Design: Callas Shortridge Architects, Culver City, CA

p. 93: (left) Photo: © Jeremy Samuelson; Design: Michaela Scherrer and Rozalynn Woods, Pasadena, CA; (bottom) Photo: Kevin Ireton, © The Taunton Press, Inc.; Design: Cass Calder Smith, San Francisco, CA

p. 94: Photos: © Joel Bennett; Design: Loren Hayden, AK

p. 95: (top) Photos: Roe A. Osborn, © The Taunton Press, Inc.; (bottom) Photos: Roe A. Osborn, © The Taunton Press, Inc.; Design: Web Wilson, Seattle, WA

p. 96: (left) Photo: © Marcia Trenary; Design: Nora Stombock, Eugene, OR; (right) Photo: © Tim Street-Porter; Design: Holger Schubert, Archisis Inc., Culver City, CA

p. 97: (top) Photo: © Mark Samu; Design: Lee Najman Interiors, Port Washington, NY; (bottom) Photo: © Roger Turk/Northlight Photography, Inc.; Design: Becky Kelleran/The Showplace Inc., Redmond, WA

p. 98: (top left) Photo: © Mark Samu, courtesy of Hearst Specials; (right and bottom) Photos: © Brian VandenBrink, Photographer 2003; Design: Morningstar Marble & Granite, Inc., Topsham, ME; Builder: Axel Berg, Falmouth, ME

p. 99: (left) Photo: © Mark Samu, courtesy of Hearst Specials; (right) Photo: © Tim Street-Porter; Design: Carol Beth Cozen, Cozen Architecture, Manhattan Beach, CA

p. 100: (left) Photo: © Tim Street-Porter; (right) Photos: © Mark Samu, courtesy of Hearst Specials

p. 101: (top) Photo: © Tim Street-Porter; (bottom) Photo: Photo courtesy Kohler Co.

p. 102: Photo: © 2003 carolynbates.com; Design: Cushman & Beckstrom, Inc., Architecture and Planning, Stowe, VT; Tile: Mark Foye, J&M Flooring, Westbrook, ME

p. 104: (left) Photo: Photo courtesy of Toto USA; (right) Photo: © davidduncanliv-ingston.com; Design: Lamperti Associates, San Rafael, CA

p. 105: (left) Photo: © 2003 carolyn-bates.com; courtesy Billings Farm & Museum, Woodstock, VT; (right) Photo: Jared Polesky; Design: Linda Beaumont/-Yestermorrow School, Warren, VT; Builder: Steven Badanes, Jared Polesky, and Brian Nesin

p. 106: (left, top right) Photos: © david-duncanlivingston.com; (bottom right) Photo: © Roger Turk/Northlight Photography, Inc.; Design: Gelotte Architects, Kirkland, WA

p. 107: (top) Photo: © 2003 carolyn-bates.com; Design: Peter Morris Architects, Vergennes, VT; (bottom) Photo: Charles Miller, © The Taunton Press, Inc.; Design: Steven Vanze/Barnes Vanze, Washington, DC

p. 108: Photo: © 2003 carolynbates.com; Design: Glenn Meade, Boston, MA

p. 109: (top) Photo: Charles Miller, © The Taunton Press, Inc.; Design: House + House Architects, San Francisco, CA; (bottom) Photo courtesy of Toto USA

p. 110: (left) Photo: Charles Miller, © The Taunton Press, Inc.; Design: House + House Architects, San Francisco, CA; (top right) Photo: © 2003 carolynbates.com; Design: Cushman & Beckstrom, Inc., Architecture and Planning, Stowe, VT; (bottom right) Photo: Charles Miller, © The Taunton Press, Inc.; Design: David Edrington, Eugene, OR

p. 111: (top left) Photo: Kevin Ireton, © The Taunton Press, Inc.; (bottom right) Photo: Courtesy Briggs Plumbing Products, Inc. ; (right) Photo courtesy of Toto USA

p. 112: (top left) Photo: © 2003 carolyn-bates.com; Design, Builder: Birdseye Building Company, Richmond, VT; (top right) © Brian VandenBrink, Photographer 2003; Design: John Silverio Architect, Lincolnville, ME; (bottom) Photo: © 2003 carolynbates.com; Design: Ted Montgomery, Indiana Architecture, Charlotte, VT

p. 113: (top, center) Photos: © Jeremy Samuelson; (bottom) Photo: © 2003 car-olynbates.com; Design, Builder: Sheppard Custom Homes, Williston, VT

p. 114: (top) Photo: © Mark Samu; Design: Bruno Haase/The Tile Studio, Merrick, NY; (bottom) Photo: © Brian VandenBrink, Photographer 2003; Design: Mark Hutker & Associates, Architects, Inc., Vineyard Haven, MA

p. 115: (left) Photo: © Brian VandenBrink, Photographer 2003; Design: Christina Oliver Interiors, Newton, MA; Architect: Allen Freysinger, Architects, Milwaukee, WI; (right top) Photo: © Mark Samu; Design: Sherrill Canet Interiors Ltd., New York, NY; (right bottom) Photo: © 2003 carolynbates.com; Design: Cushman & Beckstrom, Inc., Architecture and Planning, Stowe, VT

p. 116: (left) Photo: © Roger Turk/Northlight Photography, Inc.; Design: Sandy's Design & Remodeling, Kirkland, WA; (top right) Photo: Kevin Ireton, © The Taunton Press, Inc.; Design: Stephen Bobbitt, Seattle, WA; (bottom right) Photo: © Tim Street-Porter

p. 117: (left) Photo: © Brian VandenBrink, Photographer 2003; Design: Drysdale Associates Interior Design, Washington, DC; (right) Photo: © Jason McConathy; Design: Susan Taublieb of Rumpelstiltskins, Greenwood Village, CO

p. 118: (left top) Photo: Charles Bickford, © The Taunton Press, Inc.; Design: Paul MacNeely, Jeremiah Eck Architects, Boston, MA ; Sink: Henry Miller, Boston, MA; (left bottom) Photo: Kevin Ireton, © The Taunton Press, Inc.; Design: Cass Calder Smith, San Francisco, CA; (right) Photo: Andy Engel, © The Taunton Press, Inc.; Design: Mark Primack, Santa Cruz, CA

p. 119: Photo: Charles Miller, © The Taunton Press, Inc.

p. 120: (left) Photo: Charles Bickford, © The Taunton Press, Inc.; Design: Shahn Torontow and Ross Johnson, Victoria, B.C.; (right) Photo: Charles Miller, © The Taunton Press, Inc.; Design: Anni Tilt-Arkin/Tilt Architects, Albany, CA

p. 121: (left top) Photo: © Mark Samu, courtesy of Hearst Specials; Design: Peter Cook Architect, Southampton, NY; (left bottom) Photo: © Mark Samu; Design: Lee Najman Interiors, Port Washington, NY; (right) Photo: Scott Gibson, © The Taunton Press, Inc.; Design: James Cameron Build/Design, Pittsboro, NC

p. 122: (top) Photo: © Brian VandenBrink, Photographer 2003; (bottom) Photo: © Mark Samu; Design: Douglas Moyer Architect, Sag Harbor, NY

p. 123: (left top)Photo: © Brian VandenBrink, Photographer 2003; Design: Bruce Norelius, Elliott & Elliott Architecture, Blue Hill, ME; (left bottom) Photo: © Jason McConathy; Design: Kristi Dinner/KD Design, Denver, CO; (right) Photo: © Jason McConathy; Design: Steve & Betty Nickel/-The Portfolio Group, Estes Park, CO; Cabinet: Norman Custom Cabinets, Fort Collins, CO

p. 124: (top) Photo: © Mark Samu; Design: Douglas Moyer Architect, Sag Harbor, NY; (bottom) Photo: © 2003 carolynbates.com; Design: Kent Eaton/M. B. Cushman Design, Stowe, VT; Builder: D. A. Day Woodworking, Stowe, VT

p. 125: (top left) Photo: © Mark Samu, courtesy of Hearst Specials; (top right) Photo: © Mark Samu, courtesy of Hearst Specials; (bottom left) Photo: © Mark Samu; Design: John Hummell/Hummell Construction, East Hampton, NY; (bottom right) Photo: © davidduncanliving-ston.com

p. 126: (top) Photo: Charles Miller; Design: David Edrington, Eugene, OR; (bottom left) Photo: © Mark Samu; Design: Ellen Roche Architects, Oyster Bay, NY; (bottom right) Photo: © Brian VandenBrink, Photographer 2003; Design: Morningstar Marble, Topsham, ME
p. 127: (top left) Photo: © Tim Street-Porter; Design: Carol Beth Cozen, Cozen Architecture, Manhattan Beach, CA; (top right) Photo: © Mark Samu, courtesy of Hearst Specials; (bottom) Photo: © Tim Street-Porter; Design: Rob Quigley, San Diego, CA
p. 128: (top) Photo: © Brian VandenBrink, Photographer 2003; Design: Morningstar Marble, Topsham, ME; (center) Photo: © Mark Samu; Design: Jeanne Leonard Interiors, West Hampton Beach, NY; (bottom) Photo courtesy of Kohler Co.
p. 129: (top & bottom left) Photos: © david-duncanlivingston.com; (right) Photo courtesy of Kohler Co.

CHAPTER: 5
p. 130: Photo: © Brian VandenBrink, Photographer 2003; Design: Mary Louise Gertler, McMillen Inc., New York, NY
p. 132: Photo: © Mark Samu, courtesy of Hearst Specials
p. 133: (top left) Photo: © 2003 carolyn-bates.com; Design: Wendy Kohn, Denver, CO; (bottom left) Photo: © Mark Samu; Design: Jeanne Leonard Interiors, West Hampton Beach, NY; (right) Photo: © Brian VandenBrink, Photographer 2003; Design: Sholz & Barclay Architects, Camden, ME
p. 134: Photo: © Tim Street-Porter; Design: Korpinan–Erickson Inc., Santa Barbara, CA
p. 135: (top) Photo: © Brian VandenBrink, Photographer 2003; Design: Morningstar Marble, Topsham, ME; (bottom) Photo: © Roger Turk/Northlight Photography Inc.; Design: Gelotte Architects, Kirkland, WA
p. 136: (top) Photo: Scott Gibson, © The Taunton Press, Inc.; Design/Builder: Scott Gibson, © The Taunton Press, Inc.; (bottom) Photo: © Tim Street-Porter
p. 137: (top) Photo: © Jeremy Samuelson; (bottom) Photo: © davidduncanliving-ston.com; Design: McDonald & Moore, Ltd., San Jose, CA
p. 138: (left & right) Photos: © Mark Samu; Design: The Tile Studio, Merrick, NY
p. 139: (top & bottom) Photo: Charles Miller, © The Taunton Press, Inc.; Design: Beth Coleman, Ellison Bay, WI
p. 140: (left) Photo: © Tim Street-Porter; (top right) Photos: © Mark Samu; Design: Richard L. Schlesinger Interiors, Huntington, NY; (bottom right) Photo: ©Jeremy Samuelson
p. 141: (top) Photo: © Tim Street-Porter; Design: William Hefner, Los Angeles, CA; (bottom) Photo: © Tim Street-Porter
p. 142: (left) Photo: © Brian VandenBrink, Photographer 2003; Design: Mark Hutker & Associates, Architects, Inc., Vineyard Haven, MA; (right) Photo: © Robert Perron Photographer; Design: Paul Bierman-Lytle; Builder: Mike Costerisan

p. 143: (left) Photo: © davidduncanliv-ingston.com; (right) Photo: Charles Miller, © The Taunton Press, Inc.; Design: Bentley & Churchill, Architects, Siasconset, Nantucket, MA; Builder: Michael Phillips Construction, Nantucket, MA
p. 144: (top) Photo: © 2003 carolynbates.com; Design: M. B. Cushman Design, Stowe, VT; Builder: D. A. Day Woodworking, Stowe, VT; (bottom) Photo: © Peter Vanderwarker; Builder: Donelan Contracting
p. 145: Photo: © Lee Brauer Photography; Design:Chris McCray and Rick Farinholt; Builder: Franko, LaFratta and Farinholt, Richmond, VA
p. 146: (left) Photo: © Jeremy Samuelson; Design: Jay Griffith, Venice, CA; (top right) Photo: © National Kitchen & Bath Association, photo by Cheryl Macy; Design: Rhonda Knoche, Neil Kelly Designers/Remodelers, Portland, OR; (bottom right) Photo: ©Jeremy Samuelson
p. 147: (left) Photo: © Randi Baird; Builder: Billy Dillon/John Abrams Builders, Martha's Vineyard, MA; (right) Photo: © Mark Samu; Design: Sam Scofield Architects, Stowe, VT
p. 148: (left) Photo: © Mark Samu; Design: Val Florio Architects, Sag Harbor, NY; Builder: Hummell Construction, East Hampton, NY; (top right) Photo: © Mark Samu; Design: Daniel Barsanti/Healing Barsanti, Inc., New York, NY; (bottom right) Photo: © Todd Caverly/Brian VandenBrink Photographs; Design: Whipple Callender, Architects, Portland, ME
p. 149: (left) Photo: © Tim Street-Porter; Design: Darrell Schmitt, Los Angeles, CA; (right) Photo: © Mark Samu, courtesy of Hearst Specials
p. 150: (left) Photo: © Mark Samu, courtesy of Hearst Specials; (right) Photo: © david-duncanlivingston.com
p. 151: (left) Photo: © davidduncanliving-ston.com; Design: House + House Architects, San Francisco, CA; (right) Photo: © davidduncanlivingston.com

CHAPTER: 6
p. 152: Photo: © Mark Samu, courtesy of Hearst Specials
p. 154: (top) Photo: © 2003 carolynbates.com; Design: Peter Morris Architects, Vergennes, VT; (bottom) Photo: © 2003 carolynbates.com; Design: Truex Cullins & Partners Architects, Burlington, VT
p. 155: (left) Photo: © Jeremy Samuelson; (right) Photo: © Brian VandenBrink, Photographer 2003; Builder: Tom Hampson, Boothbay, ME
p. 156: (left) Photo: Scott Gibson, © The Taunton Press, Inc.; Design: William F. Roslansky, Woods Hole, MA; (right) Photo: © 2003 carolynbates.com; Design: David Carse/Hart Hill Design, Hinesburg, VT
p. 157: (top) Photo: © Jeremy Samuelson; Design: Tim Clarke Inc., Los Angeles, CA

p. 158: (left) Photo: © Brian VandenBrink, Photographer 2003; Design: Jeremy Moser, Architect, Portland, ME; (right) Photo: © Brian VandenBrink, Photographer 2003; Design: Mark Hutker & Associates, Architects, Inc., Vineyard Haven, MA
p. 159: (top) Photo: © Jeremy Samuelson; Design: Celia Tejada, San Francisco, CA; (bottom) Photo: Charles Bickford, © The Taunton Press, Inc.; Design: Keith Moskow, Boston, MA
p. 160: (left) Photo: © Claudio Santini Photographer, www.claudiosantini.com; Design: House + House, San Francisco, CA; (top right) Photo: © davidduncanliv-ingston.com; (bottom right) Photo: © Brian VandenBrink, Photographer 2003; Design: Morningstar Marble, Topsham, ME; Builder: Axel Berg, Falmouth, ME
p. 161: (top) Photo: Charles Miller, © The Taunton Press, Inc.; Design: © Steve Badanes/Jersey Devil; Tile: Linda Beaumont, Seattle, WA; (bottom) Photo: © Todd Caverly/Brian VandenBrink Photographs
p. 162: (top & bottom) Photos: © david-duncanlivingston.com
p. 163: (top) Photo: © davidduncanliving-ston.com
p. 164: Photo: © Mark Samu, courtesy of Hearst Specials
p. 165: (top) Photo: Charles Miller, © The Taunton Press, Inc.; Design: David Edrington, Eugene, OR; (bottom) Photo: Chris Green
p. 166: Photo: © Roger Turk/Northlight Photography, Inc.; Design: Gelotte Architects, Kirkland, WA
p. 167: (left) Photo: © 2003 carolyn-bates.com; Design: Wendy Kohn, Denver, CO; (top right) Photo: Charles Miller, © The Taunton Press, Inc.; Design: Bentley & Churchill, Architects, Siasconset, Nantucket, MA; Builder: Michael Phillips Construction, Nantucket, MA; (bottom right) Photo: © David Edrington, Architect; Design: David Edrington, Architect, Eugene, OR